MW00479940

Praise for *The Includers*

"Stronger together is not just a motto; it's a moral imperative for our success and survival. Colette Phillips has been a
passionate advocate for the values of diversity, inclusion, and
equality in her personal and professional life. Colette's inspir-
ing new book, *The Includers*, provides an important guide on
how each of us can match our ideals with our actions. In *The
Includers*, Colette Phillips demonstrates how when we reach
for the best in us, we will find the gold that enriches all of
us. *The Includers* is a must-read for those who want to build
a future that will allow us to flourish as individuals and as a
compassionate, humane, and, yes, successful society."

**—William S. Cohen, president and CEO of the Cohen
Group, and Janet Langhart Cohen, president and
CEO of Langhart Communications and author of *My
Life in Two Americas* and *Anne and Emmett***

"*The Includers* shares with a broad audience the guidance,
wisdom, and perspective that Colette has offered to me and so
many other leaders seeking to create a more inclusive workplace. Filled with insight, data, and best practices, it's the
thoughtful, tactical guide we all need to better understand and
practice allyship and create a strong organizational culture."

—Sam Kennedy, Boston Red Sox president and CEO

"*The Includers* is a call to action for all of us. Colette Phillips
is a master at bringing people together and has been an instrumental partner helping me lead our company wide DEI efforts.
Her ideas and approaches have changed the way I think about

ensuring that every employee in our business feels a sense of total belonging."

—**Thomas Bartlett, president and CEO of American Tower**

"Colette Phillips's wisdom is personally and professionally transformative. *The Includers* provides insightful stories and practical strategies that empower and embolden leaders across sectors and industries to become effective, culturally savvy, and inclusive allies. The themes and vignettes are carefully curated for insight and impact. *The Includers* is a culture-changing, narrative-shifting, and indispensable guide that should be required reading for today's leaders and changemakers."

—**Ivan Espinoza-Madrigal, executive director of Lawyers for Civil Rights**

"*The Includers* is a wise and much-needed handbook for a workplace culture of inclusion from a much-honored leader who exemplifies it. Colette Phillips weaves together her personal history, practical action tips, stories of role-model white male allies, and corporate policy ideas into a fascinating and compelling read."

—**Rosabeth Moss Kanter, professor at Harvard Business School and author of *Confidence, Confidence* and *Think Outside the Building***

"Employers, managers, and business leaders can learn a lot from the lessons and principles Colette provides in these pages. And for those who learn by doing, there's no better blueprint than to follow in the footsteps of the seven "Super Includers" whom she profiles here. This is a book that provides inspiration as much as it requires of its reader the determination to answer the call in support of diversity, equity, and inclusion."

—**Doug Banks, executive editor of *Boston Business Journal* and *Providence Business First***

"*The Includers* is a must-read filled with humanity, wisdom, and no-nonsense actions that CEOs, nonprofit executives, community leaders—in fact, every one of us—can take to rid America of its legacy of racism and sexism. This is not your typical how-to book by an academic, analyst, or consultant. Colette Phillips taps decades of her experience lifting others. She shines the light on leaders who walk the talk of inclusivity and opportunity for everyone. Her passion and prescription for a post-racist, post-sexist America comes from her heart, head, and hard-won learning about how we get there. Colette shows that our actions to advance others enriches our own well-being, too."

—Evelyn Murphy, former Massachusetts lieutenant governor, founder and president of the Wage Project, and author of *Getting Even*

"We need more books like *The Includers*, a powerful call to action for any business or community leader, that don't preach but rather teach the importance of allyship and DEI both in the workplace and at home. A master at bringing people together, Colette Phillips will inspire you to change the way you think and give you the tools you need to become an 'includer.'"

—Chris Vogel, editor of *Boston* magazine

"Colette Phillips has always had a way with words; encouraging us to act with character, courage, and compassion and to be attuned to and appreciative of cultural nuances. Her seven traits may seem like a lengthy checklist but they are all related; begin with one and you will have access to all. Her ideas have been tested and widely implemented; they impact the bottom line humanely. Turn to any section of the book and your thinking will be challenged, refreshed, or expanded. There are hundreds of real-world and commonsense examples based on Colette's lived experiences and the reality of the leaders profiled. Her insights and advice will accelerate your ability to create a compassionate and sustainable organization."

—Dr. Priscilla H. Douglas, executive coach
and author of *Woke Leadership*

"For allies looking to improve equity and inclusivity in their workplace, community, or personal life, *The Includers* is the perfect place to begin. Colette is an encouraging and clear guide for anyone ready to work for a more compassionate and connected world."

—Dr. M. Lee Pelton, president and CEO of The Boston
Foundation and president emeritus of Emerson College

"A must-read for managers and other business leaders! Colette Phillips's seven principles are a clear-cut approach to creating a collaborative, culturally intelligent workplace that supports opportunity and access for everyone."

—Rachel Pacheco, PhD, author of *Bringing Up the Boss*

The
Includers

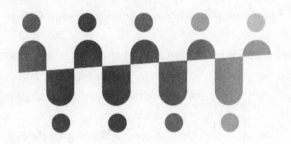

The
Includers

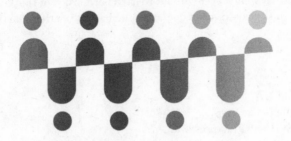

THE 7 TRAITS OF
CULTURALLY SAVVY,
ANTI-RACIST LEADERS

Colette A. M. Phillips

BenBella Books, Inc.

Dallas, TX

BenBella

BenBella Books, Inc.
10440 N. Central Expressway
Suite 800
Dallas, TX 75231
benbellabooks.com
Send feedback to feedback@benbellabooks.com
BenBella is a federally registered trademark.

Printed in the United States of America
10 9 8 7 6 5 4 3 2 1

Library of Congress Control Number: 2023025934
ISBN 9781637741382 (hardcover)
ISBN 9781637741399 (electronic)

Editing by Vy Tran and Joe Rhatigan
Copyediting by Leah Baxter
Proofreading by Rebecca Maines and Lisa Story
Indexing by Amy Murphy
Text design and composition by Aaron Edmiston
Cover design by Linet Huamán Velásquez
Cover image © Shutterstock / Nanzeeba
Printed by Lake Book Manufacturing

Special discounts for bulk sales are available.
Please contact bulkorders@benbellabooks.com.

This book is dedicated to my beloved parents, Ionie Francis Phillips and D. A .R. Phillips, who were two pioneering entrepreneurs and business leaders on the island of Antigua. They taught me acceptance, love for family and humanity, faith, and the importance of always striving to make a difference.

Contents

Foreword

Boston power has been largely white and male—until now. From City Hall to C-suites, change has arrived.

In no small part, this is because of Colette Phillips, who first came to the city over four decades ago as a seventeen-year-old college student from Antigua. She saw what Boston could become: a place where everyone could have a seat at the table. It was radical thinking, especially in a city where, for years, power had been concentrated in the hands of a group of businessmen known as the Vault.

To know Colette is to know that nothing deters her. She forged her own path, launching a public relations firm, and as a Black woman doing business in Boston, she has often been the "only" in the room. Long before the racial reckoning that followed the murder of George Floyd, Colette used her formidable communications skills—first honed at Emerson College, where she studied broadcast journalism—to impress upon companies and chief executives why diversity matters.

Not only have clients benefited from Colette's counsel, but so has all of Boston. She bridged business, civic, and political circles, and then sought to connect us all. She empowered professionals of color more than a decade ago with the launch of Get Konnected!, which has grown into a premier networking resource in Boston. However, it wasn't enough for leaders of color to get to know each other; Colette wanted the rest of the city to know their names too. So she created and publicized lists of influential people of color, many of whose profiles have only grown larger after being on her radar.

Perhaps when we look back, these lists represented a turning point in Boston because they showed what's possible. That Boston wasn't a city that needed to focus on attracting professionals of color but rather to acknowledge they were already here. There have been other organized efforts through the years to push local companies to diversify their hiring, recruiting, and promotion of people of color. But Colette's GK! lists recognized the contributions of professionals of color—long before the rest of the city even knew their names.

Consider who has appeared on *Boston* magazine's list of the 100 Most Influential Bostonians up until recently. In a city where people of color have been in the majority since 2000, the list has been predominantly white. However, in 2022, the magazine's list had forty people of color, and twenty-five of them had appeared previously on GK!'s Most Influential list.

In part, this book was inspired by one of Colette's lists: a collection of twelve white male allies in different industries that she identified as advancing diversity and inclusion in Boston. Controversial? A bit. But Colette got our attention when she explained how creating an inclusive Boston requires "white men who can jump." This is one of the biggest insights she has gleaned over a long career: An anti-racist agenda takes root when leaders take diversity seriously.

And like it or not, white men are still in charge. We can make them feel guilty or we can remind them that they—perhaps more than anyone—can change the game. Colette believes that many people want to build inclusive organizations, but they just don't know how or even where to start. Her book is instructive and unique in that it showcases white male leaders who have made or are making a difference so others can learn from and emulate them. Some of them are household names like Prince Harry; others are not, like Boston hotelier Paul Sonnabend.

Colette was working for Paul's Royal Sonesta Hotel in Cambridge in the 1980s when she decided she wanted to start her own PR firm. She told Paul of her plans and asked that Sonesta become her first client. She figured she had nothing to lose since she was leaving anyway; she would either be fired or gain her first account.

What happened next surprised her—and embodies what white male allyship is all about. Not only did Sonesta become her first client, but Paul allowed Colette to use her old office to launch her business. Colette shares Paul's story to highlight the role of courage in inclusive leadership. Rather than view Colette's departure as a threat, Paul saw it as an opportunity to support an underrepresented business owner.

Courage is among the seven Cs Colette outlines in her book: character, cultural intelligence, connections, communications, collaboration, courage, and commitment. These are the traits that have defined inclusive leaders and led them to build diverse workforces, ultimately helping them grow their bottom lines.

It is fitting that Colette's book arrives just as Boston emerges on the national stage as a place where leadership finally reflects the diverse city it has become. During the last mayoral election (2021), there was not a single viable white male candidate; in fact, all the top contenders were women of color. In the end, Boston elected Michelle Wu, its first woman and Asian American mayor, who replaced another first, Kim Janey, a Black woman who had been serving as acting mayor.

It is also fitting that Colette is playing a significant role in reshaping Boston's image to the world as part of the team that won the contract to deliver the city's first tourism campaign. The campaign is called All Inclusive Boston, and it's designed to undo the decades-old image of Boston as a racist city and make the city a destination for all people.

There is no single path to achieving diversity, equity, and inclusion. We still have a long way to go. But in this book, Colette shows us a way forward, one that requires white men who can jump and shoot . . . but also learn how to pass the ball into different hands.

—SHIRLEY LEUNG

Business Columnist and Associate Editor at the Boston Globe

Inclusion, Pandemics, and America's Racial Awakening

Several decades ago, as I was preparing to launch my PR agency, I had lunch with a friend, a columnist for the Boston edition of *Adweek*. He was a veteran of the city's PR world, and I wanted to get his perspective on whether he thought a Black-owned public relations and marketing agency would do well in Boston.

I'll never forget his response. He looked me dead in the eye and told me, in no uncertain terms, that Boston was not a city that would be supportive of or welcoming to a minority-owned business.

He said, "Colette, you are a sweet little island girl . . . why do you want to put yourself through all that frustration? You would be better off getting a job in the marketing department of a local company."

He then advised me to talk to Kendall Nash, the owner of WILD, the only Black radio station in Massachusetts at the time. He suggested that Kendall would tell me how difficult it had been for him to even get the Boston community to purchase advertising on his station.

In retrospect, I don't believe my friend's advice was ill-intended. I believe that, in his mind, he was giving me a sober dose of reality and trying to help me avoid inevitable frustration and heartbreak. Thankfully, I didn't let his advice discourage me. As the first person of color in Boston to launch a successful public relations and marketing firm, I've helped reduce barriers to entry and lessen anxiety in the marketing and communications field for other people of color.

But that conversation gave me an early preview into how hard it is for Black people to break into the halls of power, the resilience and initiative that doing so requires, and how often even the most well-meaning white people don't realize the impact of their words or actions.

I came to Boston in the early seventies as a seventeen-year-old Black girl from the small Caribbean island of Antigua. Studying communications at Emerson

College, I had high hopes and great expectations. I had done my research at the public library back home and was convinced Boston was not as racially divided and explosive as I had read the American South was. After all, it was intellectual and wealthy, the home of Harvard and the Kennedys. Dr. Martin Luther King Jr. went to the Boston University School of Theology, where he met his wife. The first man to die in the American Revolution was a Black Bostonian, and the 54th Regiment in the Civil War—the only nonwhite regiment in the war—was based in Boston.

And it was very British, particularly Back Bay, where my school was located. Having grown up in a British colonial-influenced culture myself, I truly thought I would fit in nicely in Boston, without giving any thought to race.

Boy, was I in for a rude awakening. The images on the nightly news of angry white parents and terrified Black children being bused into white communities—all being ginned up by outspoken racists like Boston school committee member Pixie Palladino and councilwoman Louise Day Hicks—told a very different story. It wasn't long before I realized that the neighborhoods featured in these news stories—South Boston, Charlestown, the North End, and East Boston—were, for all intents and purposes, off-limits to Black people.

Certainly, a lot has changed since those days. Today, my public relations office is in Charlestown. In 2021, two women of color became mayors of Boston—City Council President Kim Janey, a Black woman, ascended to the role when the sitting mayor became US Labor Secretary, and Michelle Wu became the first woman, person of color, and Asian American elected to the role. And the city council itself is no longer all white, Irish men, but rather 70 percent people of color—a reflection of changing demographics and the broader environment.

And it's not just Boston that's changed. Before the end of this century, non-Hispanic whites will no longer make up the majority of the United States' population. Fully 85 percent of all new entrants in the American workforce are women, people of color, or immigrants. And the combined buying power of Black Americans, Asian Americans, and Native Americans is estimated to be $2.4 trillion, while the nation's Hispanics command $1.5 trillion in spending power—larger than the GDP of Australia. In fact, Black buying power alone has seen impressive gains since the end of the last economic downturn, jumping from $961 billion in 2010 to an estimated $1.3 trillion in 2018.

These demographic trends indicate America will increasingly need to depend on the talents and abilities of nonwhites and women to compete in the global marketplace. However, America's corporate environment and communities still tend to see people who look and/or speak differently as a threat instead of as an asset to competing in a global economy. As a result, we are still too rarely offered a seat at the table—and that's a problem for corporate America.

A story (and possible urban legend) about a Perdue chicken ad illustrates this perfectly. Company president and CEO Frank Perdue made famous the slogan, "It takes a tough man to make a tender chicken." However, when it was translated to Spanish for an advertising campaign, billboards all over Mexico carried a photo of Perdue with one of his birds that read, "It takes a hard man to make a chicken affectionate." Had a Hispanic/Latino person been in the room to provide cultural understanding and an adequate translation, this faux pas would have been avoided.

As I built my PR company on the premise of helping companies understand and actualize the competitive advantage of inclusion, I realized something: *You can't have inclusion if you exclude the very people who have the power to make systemic changes at the corporate, societal, and philanthropic level—those who control who gets in the door, who moves up the ladder, who shares the wealth, and who gets treated like an equal.*

Ninety-nine times out of a hundred, these people—the occupants of corporate C-suites; the major political movers and shakers; the gatekeepers who oversee policy, government, sports, arts, and entertainment—are white men.

I certainly understand why many white men feel threatened by diversity. In part, it's because they fear they will end up being excluded and irrelevant as a result. But the longer I've worked in this business, the clearer it has become that there are also white men who see things differently.

Some white men use their power and their actions—in very public and very private ways—to expand the circle of people in power as well as invite those who in the past have been excluded.

There's Lyndon B. Johnson, who transformed from a congressman who ran on a white supremacy platform to leading the most sweeping civil rights reforms in American history. Or Wayland Hicks, a white male Xerox executive who mentored Ursula Burns, the first African American woman to head a Fortune 500 company as chairman and CEO of Xerox.

And there are executives like Bob Rivers, the chairman and CEO of the New England regional Eastern Bank, who made it his mission to "make sure the next generation of Boston's leaders don't look anything like him."

I call them "White Men Who Can Jump," playing off the title of the Ron Shelton basketball movie *White Men*

Can't Jump. I call them that not because they play basket-ball, but because they are leaders who aren't limited by their skin color, background, and self-interest. Contrary to stereotypes of white behavior, these men recognize the importance of diversity and inclusion to all of us—and they do something about it.

Why White Men? And Why Me?

As you read this book, you'll probably ask yourself: "How exactly did a Black Antiguan woman end up becoming a champion for white male allies?"

I've asked myself this question many times over the years! And I know it opens me up to accusations that I am an Aunt Thomasina—an apologist for racism along the lines of Candace Owens, Kanye West, or others who have found it convenient, for whatever reason, to make excuses for white male misbehavior.

But if you know me and my life or follow me on LinkedIn or Facebook, you know that I call it like I see it.

I remember once while shopping at a high-end retailer, I was waiting at the counter for a woman to assist me. She paid me no attention for a few minutes, but when a white woman walked up behind me, the saleswoman asked her if she needed help. Immediately, I said, "Excuse me. I believe I was here first." When the woman in back of me agreed, I said to the saleswoman, "I am not invisible."

When the saleswoman finally awarded me her attention, I made her work for the sale, showing me many different items before I made my selections. But when it came time for me to present my credit card to her, I paused and told her, "I don't think I want to give you this sale." I walked up to a different salesperson, handed her my items and my credit card, and had her take care of the sale. I had decided that there was no way I was going to reward bad behavior.

I'm not an apologist. But I am a pragmatist. If, as Black people, we want to shatter individual, institutional, and systemic racism . . . well . . . I don't believe that can be accomplished by Black people alone. We need to engage white allies, and especially white male allies—those who occupy the seats of power and spheres of influence where decisions get made and policy gets created. If we want to end systemic racism, it's going to take white men. Why? Because they hold that power.

"Two Gay Men and a Black Immigrant Woman Walk into a Bar . . ."

I'm also someone who believes her own eyes—and I've seen and experienced firsthand the power white men have to open doors and create access.

I didn't learn this from a captain of industry or a son of privilege, but rather two middle-aged, gay, white men who took me under their wing when I was in my mid-twenties.

Norman Pellerin and Mark Skiffington were long-time partners who lived together on Marlborough Street between Fairfield and Exeter, in a lovely quaint apartment with wonderful bay windows that looked out on Boston's Back Bay. Norman worked in design, while Mark worked in operations for John Hancock Financial. I met them while I was doing PR for the Girl Scouts—Norman worked for the company that published our monthly newsletter. He and I started chatting, and he took a liking to me. And before long, he introduced me to Mark, and they started inviting me to dinners and cocktails at their apartment.

Norman and Mark served on a number of charity committees and boards, such as for the annual galas for the Perkins School for the Blind and the Boston Lyric

Opera. Norman and Mark would invite me to these lavish events, making sure I met people who were in their circle so I didn't feel out of place or uncomfortable. People would stare at me and Norman, trying to figure out who this Black face belonged to and why she was standing alongside such a patrician, older-looking white man. Perhaps because they were gay men living in a society that was neither welcoming nor accepting of their sexual orientation, they had empathy for people of color—as I did for them.

In addition, Boston in the 1980s was very different than it is today. Long before the era of mergers and acquisitions, most of the companies that called Boston home were *actually* headquartered here. I didn't realize it at the time, but companies heavily supported the arts community—and the arts were a great way to get to know Boston's corridors of power.

Norman and Mark were on the board of the Friends of the Boston Ballet—and invited me to join.

The only requirement for sitting on this board was to be a season ticketholder and to help raise money for their signature opening-night fundraiser. I still remember that my seat was on the orchestra level, with a panoramic view of the entire theater. The feeling of being in the middle of all that was intoxicating.

Through the board and at these events, I met the wives of Boston's biggest CEOs. And I met a number of people in PR, like the late Carole Nash, the PR director for Sheraton Boston, and Patricia Petrocelli, who did PR for Filene's, the big department store that sponsored the ballet. Patricia was clever—she got Filene's to give away samples of makeup and perfume in swag bags. She used the Boston Ballet event to create visibility for Filene's—an early iteration of what we today call cause marketing. I learned a lot about the power of public relations from Carole and Patricia.

But Norman and Mark didn't just help me further my own career—they also introduced me to a number of inclusive movers and shakers, like Diddy and John Cullinane, one of the great Irish power couples in Boston.

John had made his money in tech. Diddy was from Dorchester, and both were well known in philanthropic circles for raising money for the Catholic Charities Boston. In 1989, they formed Black and White Boston Coming Together—a forty-four-person committee with equal numbers of Black and white members. Even though my company was only three years old, Diddy asked me to be one of the twenty-two Black people to serve on the committee.

At the time, Boston was in the midst of healing from the lingering busing strife of the 1970s, an economic slowdown, and the horrific 1989 murder committed by Charles Stuart, who shot and killed his pregnant wife and tried to blame a Black man. For the next twenty years, the organization brought together neighborhoods like Roxbury (a Black neighborhood) and South Boston (a white neighborhood) by encouraging participation from various sectors and people ranging from CEOs to students; supporting scholarships, speakers' series, and awards; and sponsoring a golf tournament at Franklin Park called Black and White on the Green, hosted by *Boston Globe* sports columnist Will McDonough.

Through efforts like these, I met white women leaders like Doris Yaffe, another PR director for Saks Fifth Avenue, who hosted the first-ever event by a major retailer in Boston that specifically brought together Black business and community leaders and white patrons. She held it inside Saks's flagship Boston store on Boylston Street—which until Doris's event was decidedly not a welcoming place for Black people in the 1980s.

It probably wasn't a coincidence that I was introduced to this cross-cultural work by PR people, most of whom were women. Like Carole and Patricia, Doris showed me how you could use your PR hospitality position to effect change and make a difference—attracting attention for your business while also doing good in the community. This became a model for my Get Konnected! network later on.

Serving on boards also showed me early on how I could influence these issues myself. Because of Norman and

Mark, I became the first straight woman of color to serve on the board of the AIDS Action Committee. That wasn't just for show. As a Black woman with PR skills who had grown up Christian, I could engage with Black churches that were telling their congregations that AIDS is "God's punishment." In my mind, if I was asked, "What God do you serve?" I knew it wasn't a God who loves Joseph and Mary but not Norman and Mark.

Together with nightclub impresario Patrick Lyons, the late Boston radio station Kiss 108 program director and disc jockey Sunny Joe White, and the late modeling agent Maggie Trichon, I worked to put on an annual Boston Against AIDS concert with the likes of Anita Baker, Luther Vandross (who would posthumously be outed as a gay man), and others to raise money for the AIDS Action Committee.

I have worked my tail off over the years. My friends joke that it seems like I must never sleep, but as a Black woman in business in Boston, I've perpetually felt that to achieve success, I had to work twice as hard, set a high bar for myself, and always have multiple balls in the air at once.

Ultimately, though, whether it was getting onto nonprofit boards, meeting peers and mentors in my field, or getting the chance to organize big cross-culturally significant events, none of it would have happened had

I not crossed paths with my friends Norman and Mark. They were the ones who opened the door. I learned early in my career that white male allies can create access and opportunity.

Two Pandemics

Then 2020 happened—and two pandemics.

The first was COVID-19—which quickly became a "forensic MRI on Black America" that allowed us to peek inside of Americans' lives and see the deep disparity and inequity in health care and its effect on people of color.

In the wake of the lockdowns, the *New York Times* found that Black people were three times as likely to contract COVID and twice as likely to die of the disease—not because of genetics, but because of a lack of health care, economic insecurity, and a higher likelihood of being front-line workers.[1]

Sure enough, COVID was only the first pandemic. The other? Systemic racism deeply embedded in our criminal justice system, schools, hospitals and—in some ways most importantly—in the way we do business.

Brought to light by the murder of George Floyd at the hands of a Minneapolis police officer, who kneeled on Floyd's throat for an agonizing eight minutes and forty-six seconds, this pandemic revealed just how much pain Black and brown people already faced before coronavirus even reached our shores. The result was a racial reckoning . . . and something of a eureka moment for corporate America.

Unlike after the cases of Eric Garner, Sandra Bland, or countless others who lost their lives because of police brutality, in an instant, white executives finally realized what they had been missing.

More than once during conference calls with both clients and white friends, I heard, "Black people told us this was happening to them—but I didn't believe it." After George Floyd, white America could no longer deny systemic racism—and once they saw it with the police, they could see it in their workplace. They didn't need a literal knee on the neck to see how implicit bias within their companies might be creating barriers that limit career advancement for Black people in many ways— some subtle . . . some not so subtle.

More than ever, the double pandemics of COVID and racial inequity reaffirmed the need for a more inclusive economy. But it also pointed to the need to dismantle systemic and institutional racism that has resulted in everything from drastically shorter lifespans in some neighborhoods and a quality of education more likely to be determined by zip code than grit and smarts, to unequal access to billions of dollars in state, local, and private contracts for Black-owned businesses.

THE ORGANIZATIONAL COST OF NOT EMBRACING DIVERSITY

Increasingly, we are all familiar with the benefits of diversity, equity, and inclusion (DE&I). But Includers know that in addition to the return on investment, there is a high cost to ignoring DE&I. That cost includes:

1. **Fewer Profits.** Organizations and companies that lack diversity are increasingly passed over by investors, customers, and potential employees who want to do business with companies where diversity is valued.

2. **Less Innovation.** A business model and an employee base that don't include diverse perspectives are less likely to effectively ideate and innovate.

3. **Reduced Customer/Client Base.** Ignoring the demographic shift in today's marketplace means you are also ignoring potential customers and clients who may want to do business with you.

4. **Constant Recruiting.** Organizations that fail to fully embrace and appreciate diversity suffer high turnover rates among their employees.

5. **Low Productivity.** Companies that lack diversity often have lower employee morale and are less productive.

6. **Dysfunctional Decision-Making.** Organizations that do not make diversity a core value are more prone to making knee-jerk, short-term decisions as opposed to informed, long-term strategy.

7. **Reduced Competitive Edge.** The business an organization loses due to a lack of diversity opens the door for potential competitors.

A How-To Guide for America's Anti-Racism Moment

Like few other times in our nation's history, people are not only looking at the problem of systemic racism but also for solutions. Across America, and in every aspect of our lives, Americans of all stripes—from CEOs and policymakers to town managers, school administrators, and individuals—are looking for ways to make a difference. This is our opportunity to help people not simply be "against" racism—but to actively do our part to end it. To be "anti-racists" and go from ally to advocate . . . and accomplice.

Now, this book—which I'd first envisioned in 2019—feels more necessary than ever. I wanted to write this to serve as a kind of handbook for an inclusive, more productive and equitable workplace. To help people on the journey from denial to acceptance. From thinking racism is a vague problem to seeing that it is real . . . and that they can do something about it.

After all, it wasn't until people *saw* what happened at the Edmund Pettus Bridge in Selma—when innocent unarmed Black people were beaten with batons by policemen on horses—that people understood how some police were there to serve and protect not Black people but the status quo and a system that was designed to keep Black people down.

These egregious acts captured on film—from the indelible footage and images from Selma to the cellphone videos of the policeman kneeling on the neck of George Floyd—opened people's eyes to how white privilege is weaponized and shapes our social and power structures.

I also wanted to give employers and organizations an opportunity to view everything they do through a lens of racial equity, so they do right by all their employees, set the right expectations, and ask the right questions. That way, when white executives walk into a work meeting with no people of color, they don't sit down—they ask why.

And for employees, I want to offer some ways to add value to the conversation by helping their employers create a culture of inclusion—and a workforce that values and promotes Includers.

Each chapter features one of my seven Cs: character, cultural intelligence, connections, communications, collaboration, courage, and commitment. They are lessons I've learned from counseling individuals, leaders, and institutions over the past three decades on how creating inclusive workforces—engaging employees, hiring diverse workforces, helping more people make decisions—grows your bottom line.

They're about how including people of color and diverse consumers in your business's marketing mix can help you expand your market share.

They're about why creating a communications platform that allows for broad-based buy-in—by inviting everyone to be a part of the solution—means that everybody can be treated equally and in the same way and everybody can go to work feeling like they can make a difference.

Like a doctor's prescription, the seven Cs give us the tools we all need to be anti-racist—to see how our system has been set up to benefit a certain group of people and disenfranchise others, and to do our part dismantling four hundred years of structural, systemic, and institutional racism.

In the process, I highlight Includers who have embraced these lessons—those who have had the courage, commitment, and conviction to be anti-racist advocates and accomplices when it isn't easy . . . who have demonstrated the cultural intelligence and core values to understand what is right and what is wrong, and to do something about it . . . and who employ the communications and connections necessary to really make a lasting difference at home, in the workplace, and in their communities.

CHAPTER 1

Character

CIVIL, ETHICAL LEADERSHIP COUNTS

Royal Upheaval, Regal Response

In 2017, when Prince Harry, Duke of Sussex, announced he was going to marry Meghan Markle, a biracial, divorced American actress who is the descendant of slaves, he shook more than a few teacups in Great Britain as he delivered diversity in a big way to the royal family. An ugly backlash to the engagement ensued, but Harry stood firm, and in the spring of 2018 they married. Less than two years later, in the fall of 2019, Prince Harry said in a statement, "I have been a silent witness to her private suffering for too long. To stand back and do nothing would be contrary to everything we believe in."[2]

Within a year, they would leave the British monarchy. That's character!

Things came to a head in March 2021, when Harry and Meghan sat down for an interview with Oprah Winfrey and aired what some would call "the royal dirty laundry" about the cruel and racially insensitive behavior Meghan had endured during their time together. Among the most shocking details exposed during the interview was Meghan's revelation that a family member within Buckingham Palace had expressed concerns about how dark their son Archie's skin color would be even before his birth.

No one should have been shocked by Prince Harry's choice of Meghan, an outspoken advocate for issues ranging from gender and racial equity to climate change and environmental justice, as a spouse. After all, Harry was raised by his mother to think inclusively. Princess Diana made sure that Harry and his brother, Prince William, were comfortable with people of different cultural backgrounds, leading them to enjoy visits to diverse nations and to value helping and supporting those different from them. Princess Diana also broke the rules of royal protocol. Instead of being distant in her demeanor, she hugged and touched people, and Harry carried this strong model he learned from his mother into his adulthood.

In 2004, Harry traveled to Lesotho in southern Africa, where he worked with vulnerable children, and along with that country's Prince Seeiso, he created Sentebale, a charity to help children there as well as in Botswana. A dozen years later, Harry attended the 21st International AIDS Conference in Durban, South Africa, and on World AIDS Day, he and award-winning singer and businesswoman Rihanna helped publicize HIV testing by taking tests themselves.

Prince Harry's efforts to support his spouse brought a much-needed dose of diversity awareness to the royal family and England itself—and spoke volumes about his character. Indeed, as Michelle Obama said about the presidency, power "doesn't change who you are. It reveals who you are."[3] It reveals one's character. And to be sure, we see how this can be true of people with low character—such as Bernie Madoff, who, using his power and influence, "made off" with other people's money.

But with Prince Harry, we saw something very different. Here was someone who could have had his pick of any woman. That he chose Meghan—ultimately over his own family—was a matter of character, of seeing her humanity and how she shared his values.

Why Character Matters to Being an Includer

Harry's example shows why character is the basis for being an ally in the fight for anti-racism. The values we need to fight racism and prejudice—courage, communications, compassion, connections, collaboration, cultural intelligence—all flow from the core values we are taught as children, in our home, and at school.

But how we bring our core values to the world—how we live, work, and lead—is determined by our character.

In his book *Winners Never Cheat,* multibillionaire Jon Huntsman Sr. wrote that character determines "which rules we honor and which we ignore . . . and how closely we will allow our value system to affect our lives." And in the case of anti-racism, it determines how closely our value systems will affect the lives of others.

Let's look for a moment at how inclusive leaders show character.

How the Character of Inclusive Leaders Promotes Anti-Racism

Includers Take a Side, the Right Side

Inclusive leaders demonstrate character in a variety of ways—but one of the most important is that they take a side. They don't sit silently in the face of challenge and controversy. Rather, they take responsibility and address issues despite feelings of discomfort. They do what writer Elie Wiesel implored during his 1986 Nobel Prize acceptance speech: "We must always take sides. Neutrality helps the oppressor, never the victim . . . Wherever men and women are persecuted because of their race, religion, or political views, that place must—at that moment—become the center of the universe."[4]

When Mitch Landrieu was mayor of New Orleans, he explained to the city his controversial decision to take down three monuments honoring Confederate leaders and one commemorating a violent coup against the Louisiana state government by an organization called the White League. He said, "There is a difference between remembrance of history and reverence for it."[5] What Landrieu also pointed out was that people were using these statues as a platform for discrimination, calling them their heritage. Contrary to popular belief, these monuments had not been put up in the aftermath of the

Civil War, but a hundred years after slavery had been outlawed. In my humble opinion, this had been done to intimidate Black people and instill fear in those who were powerless and had no control of legislatures.

It would have been easy for Landrieu to stay neutral on this subject. His father, also a politician, had been a huge force in the integration of New Orleans in the 1960s and '70s—and Mitch could have cloaked inaction in his father's civil rights legacy. But the Mayor of the Big Easy didn't take the easy way out. He realized children had to learn Southern history as it really happened, not as it was falsely taught in schools. For his efforts, he received a Profile in Courage Award from the John F. Kennedy Library Foundation and has since launched E Pluribus Unum, a nonprofit dedicated to dismantling the racial and class barriers that divide us.

Mitch Landrieu acknowledged what many leaders often can't: that neutrality isn't really neutral. It's wanting to be a bystander. So, he did what Includers do, and showed character by taking the side that mattered.

Includers Put Their Egos Aside

Inclusive leaders look at themselves and are willing to put their own egos aside when including women and people of color.

Now, I know what you're thinking: Most CEOs would sign their firstborn away before checking their egos at the door. This may be true. Ego is often a big part of what gets leaders to the top in the first place. Many of them become so successful that they believe they can change things by their sheer force of will.

Inclusive leaders are wired a little differently, though. To be sure, they have an ego, but they temper it with reflection and introspection. They recognize they may not know all the answers and are willing to listen.

My favorite example of this was when Wayland Hicks, a white male Xerox executive, came face-to-face with Ursula Burns, a Black entry-level engineer making $30,000 a year. It was 1989, and Hicks was leading a company forum on work-life balance. When a colleague asked him whether diversity initiatives were lowering hiring standards, Hicks simply stated it wasn't true. But Burns, clearly dissatisfied with his meager response, stood up in front of everyone and let Hicks know she was disappointed he hadn't more forcefully dismissed the notion out of hand.

Hicks reproached Burns for her tone. But instead of firing her or reprimanding her because she had embarrassed him, he did something very different: He continued their conversation over several meetings. In time, Hicks offered her a role that introduced her to the C-suite and changed the course of her career—and American business. Eventually, Burns would go on to become CEO of Xerox and the first Black female CEO to head a Fortune 500 company.[6]

What makes that story powerful was Hicks's ability to put his ego aside and allow himself to see beyond a disagreement in front of his peers and subordinates to recognize Burns's talent, hard work, and initiative—even though these two people couldn't have been more different. Burns had grown up in a single-parent household in the projects on New York City's Lower East Side and was working as an entry-level engineer. Hicks was a senior-level executive who had held several executive positions within the company—"a company man." Yet, this company man allowed himself to take an interest in Burns and guide her in how to use her boldness and abilities to stand up for what she believed in and to foster a career she and others would be proud of.

There are countless other examples of white male executives mentoring talented people of color and women toward leadership. Some have even groomed their successors. Bob Rivers, Chairman and CEO of Boston's Eastern Bank, chose Quincy Miller as the next President and Vice Chairman. The fourteen-member General Motors Board of Directors—eight of whom were, you guessed it, white men—unanimously appointed Mary Barra the first woman CEO of a major automobile company.

But perhaps the most obvious and recent example was presidential candidate Joe Biden's choice of Kamala Harris as his running mate. This was surprising to some, especially since in an early primary debate, she had called him out for opposing school integration busing in the 1970s . . . implying his opposition was racist. It would have been easy for Biden to use this criticism as an excuse to pass on Harris as his running mate, and there were a number of articles suggesting he would do just that. But at the end of the day, Biden didn't let his ego get in the way—just as he hadn't when Barack Obama, a senator with one-twelfth of Biden's senatorial experience, selected him to be his running mate a dozen years earlier. Little wonder he would go on to appoint the most diverse cabinet in the history of the United States.

White male allies can play a game-changing role in corporate board and senior-level actions to break down barriers, and it all begins with having the character to make decisions driven by talent and inclusivity, not ego.

Includers Accept the Criticism that Comes with Allyship

Most of us are not fond of being criticized. But criticism comes with being a leader, especially when making decisions that are right but unpopular. In the words of Dr. Martin Luther King Jr., "The ultimate measure of a man is not where he stands in moments of comfort and convenience, but where he stands at times of challenge and controversy."[7]

On April 12, 2018, two Black men waiting for a friend at a Philadelphia Starbucks were denied use of the restroom and eventually arrested because they didn't make a purchase. It became a national story.

The charges would ultimately be dropped . . . but the damage was done. Howard Schultz, Starbucks's CEO, was appalled and embarrassed. The incident threatened his cultivated reputation as an activist leader of a progressive company. But rather than get defensive, he went on the offensive. He stepped up quickly and shut down eight thousand stores for a day so that all 175,000 baristas and workers in the company could take an unconscious bias course devised with the help of attorney Bryan Stevenson's Equal Justice Initiative, the NAACP Legal Defense and Educational Fund, and the Anti-Defamation League. In addition to these trainings, Starbucks changed its policy to make all Starbucks cafés welcoming regardless of whether a purchase is made or not.

In the process, Schultz took on an incredible amount of criticism. The trainings weren't popular, even among many of his employees. While some thought the organization took the problem seriously, others saw Schultz's response as pandering, awkward, or ineffective.

But what wasn't in doubt was his sincerity. He thought training his staff was important and was willing to suffer some measure of criticism for it. That sent an important message to staff, franchisees, Black workers, and the community at large that, as Schultz said, he wanted to "lead . . . and manage the company through the lens of humanity."[8]

Includers Take Action Instead of Awaiting Perfection

Inclusive leaders also understand the power of taking action and don't wait for everything to align perfectly before doing so. They don't need to wait for a crisis—either local or national—to do the right thing and lean into issues of diversity, equity, and inclusion.

In 2017, after Donald Trump's election but before #MeToo had begun in earnest, asset management company State Street Global Advisors unveiled the *Fearless Girl* statue across from Wall Street's famous *Charging Bull*. The fifty-inch figure of a strong young girl became a huge viral sensation almost immediately. At the same time, the investment manager announced they would be using their proxy voting power as shareholders at annual meetings to vote against companies with no women on their boards. Armed with research showing women on boards were a net positive for businesses and their clients, leadership began meeting with companies to learn if they had a plan in place to add a woman director. Leading the charge for State Street Global Advisors' Fearless Girl campaign was Rakhi Kumar, a South Asian woman who headed up the company's asset stewardship division.

It wasn't long before the investment giant faced criticism, speculation about their motives, and accusations of using *Fearless Girl* as a marketing ploy. And it wasn't long before the spotlight began to shine on State Street's own record with diversity. Its board wasn't as diverse as it could have been, and it was revealed the company had settled a discrimination case with the Department of Labor, which many people thought made the company hypocritical.

But Ronald P. O'Hanley, the company's chairman and CEO, didn't back down, arguing that the firm didn't commission *Fearless Girl* because the company was perfect, and if they had waited for that, they never would have acted. Instead, despite concerns inside State Street, the company pressed forward. To clarify the company's intention, he declared, "*Fearless Girl* was never a statement of accomplishment. Her purpose is aspirational and inspirational for us and all others."[9] O'Hanley's response—and State Street's own subsequent efforts to diversify its board and leadership—is a reminder that Includers also own up to past mistakes and don't let them slow or dilute their commitment to diversity and inclusion.

I also think we should take a look at someone like Canada's Prime Minister, Justin Trudeau, who dressed up in brownface as a Middle Eastern person when he was twenty-nine and teaching at a private school. When this was revealed, rather than trying to justify it, he owned it. Trudeau admitted he was young, foolish, and wrong. By contrast, when the news came out that Governor Ralph Northam of Virginia had dressed up in blackface when he was younger (what's up with this?), he backtracked an initial apology and denied responsibility, leaving his political career in ruins.

More important than simply admitting his own mistake, though, Trudeau's life since that error has been deeply committed to diversity, inclusion . . . and action. In fact, it was Trudeau who established Canada's first ethnically diverse cabinet with an equal number of men and women, including naming Harjit Sajjan, a Sikh Indian Canadian man, his minister of defense.

These leaders prove that, as the saying goes, when you walk with purpose, you collide with destiny. By refusing to allow mistakes or imperfections to cow them into inaction or treading water, Includers demonstrate the character necessary to make progress, even when it isn't expedient.

Includers Embrace Transparent Decision-Making

Inclusive leaders also have nothing to hide when it comes to facing challenges. Honesty is important, but when it comes to inclusion, how you make decisions, and who is part of these decisions, is often as important as the decisions themselves.

If there's one thing I've learned in my thirty-year public relations career, it's that admitting vulnerability is hard for people. No one wants to be seen as a laggard or indifferent to the needs of others. So there is a tendency to minimize bad news about diversity as well as limit discussions to a need-to-know basis.

Includers approach these issues differently. They start with the idea that everyone has progress to make, and then approach the entire decision-making process in a candid and transparent way.

That's what Tim Ryan, Chairman and Senior Partner at PricewaterhouseCoopers (PwC) did. Back in 2017, he had started a group called CEO Action for Diversity & Inclusion on the belief that diversity and inclusion promote higher-quality decisions and enhance economic growth. Like a lot of companies following the murders of George Floyd, Breonna Taylor, Ahmaud Arbery, and the impact of this violence on communities of color, PwC made commitments to move faster on diversity and inclusion.

One of their most notable commitments was to be more transparent about diversity strategy and results. While they described the progress they had made, they didn't sugarcoat it—and they highlighted the need to accelerate progress in the representation of women and racial/ethnic diversity across all employee levels, do more to retain diverse teammates as they advance in their careers, and proactively place more women and racially and ethnically diverse partners in charge of leading large client engagements.

Perhaps most importantly, they recognized the importance of disclosing diversity data publicly—even though it wasn't required. In its first-ever Transparency Report, entitled "Building on a Culture of Belonging," the company wrote, "This . . . will drive visibility to the next steps on our journey. By publishing this report, we are sharing our story and holding ourselves accountable for transformative progress by sharing what has worked well and acknowledging what hasn't."[10]

Ryan also used communications channels to drive transparency, writing a blog on the company website and on LinkedIn so employees and the public alike could understand what the company was doing—and why.

Inclusive leaders don't hide challenges. They push themselves to be open and transparent about them. Includers learn to be comfortable saying they "don't know what they don't know" and accept the pressure transparency will create in order to get things right.

The Character to Make a Difference

On the road to a more inclusive, equitable business place and society, Includers are going make mistakes. They will say the wrong thing. They will sometimes do the wrong thing. But they won't let embarrassment or a bruised ego prevent them from correcting their error.

As Jon Huntsman Sr. wrote, "There are no moral shortcuts in the game of business—or life. There are, basically, three kinds of people: the unsuccessful, the temporarily successful, and those who become and remain successful. The difference is character."[11]

THE SIX PILLARS OF CHARACTER

So, what exactly goes into character? Drake University has a character education workshop program called CHARACTER COUNTS! to answer this question for educators and school systems. The goal of the program is to improve civility and develop ethical leaders. It's built on six pillars of character that were identified by a nonpartisan, secular group of youth development experts as core ethical values that transcend cultural, religious, and socioeconomic differences. And as it so happens, they are very aligned with the goals of being an Includer.

I've modified the descriptions of these pillars slightly to show how Includers can draw on these pillars in their work and communities, but the Six Pillars of Character are:

1. **Trustworthiness**
   - *Be honest. Don't deceive, cheat, or steal.*
   - *Demonstrate integrity.*
   - *Keep promises.*
   - *Be loyal.*

2. **Respect**
   - *Be accepting of differences.*
   - *Be courteous to others.*

- *Deal peacefully with anger, insults, and disagreements.*
- *Be mindful of other people's opinions and feelings.*

3. Responsibility

- *Follow through on your commitments.*
- *Show restraint.*
- *Think before you act. Consider consequences.*
- *Be accountable for your words, actions, and attitudes.*

4. Fairness

- *View all of your actions though an equity lens.*
- *Play by the rules.*
- *Leverage your privilege to give colleagues an opportunity to contribute.*
- *Be open-minded. Listen to others.*
- *Don't take advantage of others.*

5. Caring

- *Be compassionate and kind.*
- *Express gratitude.*
- *Show a tendency to forgive when people make mistakes.*

6. Citizenship

- *Commit to making your organization and community more inclusive.*
- *Cooperate and collaborate.*
- *Stand up and speak out on issues of inequity and social injustice.*
- *Make choices that protect the safety and rights of others.*
- *Create a welcoming and safe environment for everyone.*

CHAPTER 2

Cultural Intelligence

**INSIGHT AND SELF-AWARENESS TO
MITIGATE MISUNDERSTANDING**

A Professor, a Policeman,
and a President

In the summer of 2009, world-renowned Harvard professor Henry Louis "Skip" Gates Jr. was arrested for entering his own home by James Crowley, a white police officer who was investigating a robbery near the professor's Harvard Square residence in Cambridge, Massachusetts.

The story received worldwide media attention, and almost everyone had an opinion on the incident, including the Black governor of Massachusetts, Deval Patrick, the Black mayor of Cambridge, Denise Simmons, and, most famously, the Black President of the United States, Barack Obama. In a country where race and racial issues have long been very uncomfortable subjects, the nation's first Black president found himself walking on a razor's edge. At a press conference just days after the Gates-Crowley encounter, the relatively new president went on national TV and exclaimed that there must be some "teachable moments" from this incendiary event before opining that the way Officer Crowley handled the incident was "boneheaded."

Instead, a "teachable moment" became a torrent of negative comments and a backlash against the President—mostly from white Americans—for expressing his own frustration with police discrimination. In the midst of the nation's worst economic woes in a generation, this racial profiling–related incident, which had taken place in one of America's most liberal cities, took center stage. President Obama took a step. He held a "beer summit" on the White House lawn with Professor Gates and Officer Crowley in attendance.

Many dismissed the President's attempt at a détente as simplistic and not fully addressing the real issue of systemic, structural, and institutional racism. But what those critical of the President's diplomatic, if small, gesture missed was the point he was making: When people connect socially and put forth an effort to understand one another, barriers of fear and difference fade away and acceptance emerges in their place.

This is called cultural intelligence—or as I like to call it, "CQ." The scholarly study of intercultural communication dates back to the 1950s, with the work of anthropologist Edward T. Hall—though some believe it goes back even further, stemming from the research of Charles Darwin, Karl Marx, and Sigmund Freud. Regardless of the timing of its origin and who gets credit, its necessity is indisputable.

But CQ, in my view, is essential to overcoming racism. CQ is your ability to interact effectively with people across traditional social, ethnic, or racial lines. It's more than just awareness and sensitivity; it's the ability to relate to others and to work effectively with them regardless of the situation. It's also the ability to recognize the experiences of others and accept those experiences as different from your own, and in some cases, similar to or even the same as your own. For instance, in the wake of all the criticism President Obama took for his beer summit, Gates and Crowley not only went on to have an amicable relationship, but they also found out they are distant cousins and share a common Irish ancestor. They never would have discovered this without President

Obama demonstrating his own cultural intelligence and bringing them together to work on theirs.

Why Cultural Intelligence Is an Advantage

Cultural intelligence is an increasingly valuable skill for leaders, both personally and professionally. You need it when you find yourself in a new social situation, and you need it when your business opens an office in a new city or country.

America has steadily grown more diverse and is projected to be minority white by 2045. But feelings about our diversity are complicated. According to the Pew Research Center, Americans generally feel positive about our diversity, with more than half saying racial and ethnic diversity is very good for the country, and more than six in ten Americans (64 percent) reporting that the US population being made up of people of many different races and ethnicities has a positive impact on the country's culture. But even with this positive outlook, very few Americans cross racial and ethnic boundaries to regularly interact with people from other racial and ethnic groups. This includes one in four whites.

There is also increasing evidence that diverse teams spur creativity and innovation and lead to better financial performance. A study in *Harvard Business Review* found that companies "out-innovate and out-perform others" if they have "2D Diversity." That is, if they are not only culturally diverse but also have leaders with "acquired diversity."[12]

The authors say:

Acquired diversity involves traits you gain from experience: Working in another country can help you appreciate cultural differences, for example, while selling to female consumers can give you gender smarts.

Cultural intelligence can cross these boundaries in meaningful ways. It enhances your ability to be competitive in culturally diverse markets, both domestically and globally, because it allows you to interpret cultural norms and nuances of both consumers and your workforce more quickly. Cultural intelligence also makes you an employer of choice because diverse employees feel they belong and can have an impact.

Certainly, demonstrating cultural intelligence can form the basis for stronger customer relationships. After quarterback Colin Kaepernick protested police killings of

Black men by taking a knee during the national anthem, Nike's move to embrace him was highly controversial for two reasons: Older white men made up much of the NFL's fan base, and at the time, Nike was bidding on an apparel contract with the league. But Nike understood a bigger picture. The demographics of the country were changing, and therefore so was the NFL fan base. Plus, the then nascent Black Lives Matter movement was growing in impact. The company stood with Kaepernick, and then saw its sales grow and its stock price go up. Remember, Includers take sides. In the wake of George Floyd's murder in 2020 and the groundswell of popular support for BLM, Nike was effectively vindicated for its choice and rewarded for the cultural intelligence it showed by embracing, rather than eschewing, Kaepernick.

But the value of CQ is not limited to market share and bottom lines. Consider health care. Patients bring their cultural values, customs, and beliefs to the examining room. Culturally intelligent clinicians are aware of and familiar with patients' ethnicities and customs. Something as straightforward as language or the use of herbal medicine can determine the outcome of their reputation as a health care provider.

By contrast, companies with low cultural intelligence are more likely to make cultural faux pas in their business practices or even their marketing. For instance, in

1993, a magazine AT&T sent to 300,000 employees globally featured a drawing of characters from multiple continents speaking on the phone. All were human, except the character representing Africa, which was a monkey.

Workers and activists alike were understandably incensed. In its apology, AT&T expressed its dismay that "this kind of thing could have gotten by us," and pinned the blame on the artist and production manager who created the drawing.[13] But had they had a diverse creative team—or leadership with a modicum of cultural intelligence—the whole ordeal never would have happened.

Improving Your Cultural IQ

There are many culture gaps among the Black, brown, and white experiences that whites often don't even realize. Cultural intelligence can help us bridge those gaps. Institutions can use cultural intelligence not simply as a communications tool, but also to improve practices and make them more inclusive.

For instance, it's no secret that many in the Black community are more comfortable going to African American providers, in part because they don't believe health care is delivered equally to people of color.

Indeed, the health disparity between Black people and their white counterparts was exposed by COVID-19 like a forensic MRI.

To address these concerns head on, Massachusetts General Hospital—one of the leading medical institutions in the world—opened health centers in suburbs with the express purpose of addressing health disparities outside of the city, and charged the Center for Community Health Improvement's founding director, Joan Quinlan, to get it done.

Then there's Boston Medical Center, with executives like Dr. Thea L. James at the helm, which has become one of the nation's leading urban hospitals dedicated to understanding and addressing the needs of a diverse population. The medical center funds a nonprofit online platform called HealthCity that regularly updates the community on pressing health issues such as racial bias and equity, immigration, and diseases like sickle cell anemia that disproportionately impact minorities. Indeed, a number of these efforts proved critical during the COVID-19 pandemic, when these services allowed underserved populations in Boston to receive COVID testing and vaccines in more approachable, non-hospital settings within their own community.

The scientific community is still on the fence as to whether you can change your intelligence quotient.

However, the good news about your cultural intelligence is that you can improve it, no matter where you start.

If Lyndon Baines Johnson—a white supremacist who used the N-word and admitted he was oblivious to racism until he became a teacher and saw how Hispanic kids were treated—can do it, so can we. So, what else does it take?

How Inclusive Leaders Use Cultural Intelligence to Drive Diversity

Includers Do Their Homework to Show Respect for Other Cultures

It's often been said that you only get one chance to make a good first impression. CEOs generally understand this, so they rarely walk into a room and just wing it. This is particularly important when working with other cultures.

Before Dr. Peter Slavin, the recently retired President of Massachusetts General Hospital, walks into a room, he wants to know who's going to be there and what messages he is expected to deliver. He wants to be prepared to answer the tough questions, like what his hospital is doing regarding health inequities.

Leaders like Peter also work with staff ahead of time to ensure they all know what's appropriate for the audience, even including greetings: Is a nod, a handshake, or a bow preferred? He and his staff also attempt to learn which topics are appropriate to raise and which are not. For example, in some Arabic and Muslim cultures it's considered inappropriate to inquire about a man's wife, even if simply as a courtesy.

Inclusive leaders also resist the temptation to make jokes when engaging with culturally diverse audiences. In America, humor is everywhere, and is often used as a crutch when nervous. But in many other cultures, humor is considered unprofessional or disrespectful, and jokes don't always translate well cross-culturally. Inclusive leaders avoid jokes, slang, and even acronyms . . . anything that could be seen as insulting or exclusionary or make others uncomfortable.

Building a relationship means making an effort. If in doubt about what to do, look at what others are doing and have done. Discern what is the norm, and then follow suit. If you make a mistake—and you will—don't be too hard on yourself. Apologize, and get it right the next time. That will be appreciated too.

Includers Demonstrate Curiosity About Diversity and Different Cultures

Of course, sometimes we are thrust into new situations unprepared—like a meeting or a dinner with someone from a different culture than ours. Instead of telling someone about your own culture or interests, ask questions. Celebrity chef Anthony Bourdain was a natural at this. One of the reasons so many people loved his show *Parts Unknown* was because he sat with the people and got to know them culturally. He took viewers to new places—jungles, deserts, rural areas—and brought them fully inside. And because he was open and curious while breaking bread with those who lived in faraway places, those he visited revealed more about themselves and their culture than they otherwise probably would have.

Leaders can be equally deliberate. Tom Bartlett, the President and CEO at American Tower, a wireless communications company, recognized he needed to make a stronger connection with his global employee base. So, he did a series of listening tours along with his staff to engage with employees and seek their input or hear concerns. Not only that, but he also did a diversity audit and brought in an independent company to speak to employees about *their* perception of diversity at the company and where the gaps were. But he also knows there's still work to be done and has acknowledged his company still lacks racial and gender diversity on its leadership team and board. Cultural IQ is about recognizing there are gaps—cultural and gender—and making the effort to correct them.

Includers Leverage Their Own Limited Experience to Make an Authentic Connection

Leaders with an inclusive lens also use their new knowledge to express sentiments they hadn't realized before. They recognize and own their own ignorance in an attempt to connect with diverse audiences.

In 2016, then Chairman and CEO of AT&T Randall L. Stephenson gave a powerful speech about cultural intelligence at a dinner with the company's employee resource groups. This dinner took place in the wake of racial violence in Ferguson, Missouri; Charlotte, North Carolina; and Dallas, Texas, the company's headquarter city, at a time when the company had a workforce that was over 40 percent Black, had call centers throughout the South, and was hoping to win approval from the Obama administration to buy Time Warner.

During the dinner, Stephenson shared a story about how one of his best friends had never told him about the racist behavior he had faced throughout his life, and posed the question, "If two very close friends of different races don't talk openly about this issue that's tearing our communities apart, how do we expect to find common ground about what is clearly a serious problem?"[14] He went on to explain how he now realizes how much the slogan "All Lives Matter" hurts those concerned with violence against Black people in America.

That speech wasn't the last time Stephenson leveraged his own previous ignorance to discuss these issues. In the wake of George Floyd's death, he explained in a CNBC interview that he thought most white people would be surprised by how strongly their Black coworkers in the cubicles next to them felt during the protests. He also shared a story about how a Black friend had taught his children how to respond if pulled over by the police. Stephenson admitted that it never would have occurred to him to do so with his own children and that this newly found knowledge led him to urge fellow CEOs to use their power in DC to lobby for police and criminal justice reform.

Stephenson demonstrated his CQ by recognizing and legitimizing the pain his Black friends and employees were feeling. Just as important, he explained his own privilege as a white man, and shared his own efforts to seek, understand, act, and speak out regularly on the subject.

Includers Welcome Hospitality

When I was growing up in Antigua, my father used to say that you can't call someone a friend until you've broken bread with them—that there was intimacy in sharing a meal. As I've gotten older, I've seen how true that is—how you can sit next to someone whom you butted heads with all day, and then make a powerful connection, get to know them at their core, and see what they eat and drink (and maybe drink too much!).

Inclusive leaders understand this. They see how hospitality breaks down barriers and how in many cultures, friendship and family are the keys to establishing good rapport and strong business ties.

When Navjot Singh, a managing partner at McKinsey & Company, moved to Boston to start his job, he realized that he needed to build relationships. He didn't just go to lunch or take coworkers golfing. Instead, he started a monthly innovation speakers series, inviting people into his own home in Weston and feeding them. He made them feel welcome and used hospitality to build bridges.

The Power of Culture Curiosity

At the conclusion of his remarks to AT&T employees in 2016, Randall L. Stephenson explained why he believed cultural intelligence differed from simply trying to coexist or get along. "Tolerance is for cowards," he said. "Being tolerant requires nothing from you but to be quiet and not make waves, holding tightly to your views and judgments without being challenged. Do not tolerate each other. Work hard, move into uncharted territory, and understand each other."[15]

He recognized something inclusive leaders understand: that culture is a very personal thing—it shapes our values, our life trajectories, and our relationships. So, when someone makes an effort to understand another's culture, it means a lot.

As a business leader, the more people sense you are culturally intelligent, the more willing they will be to open up, allowing you to function more effectively in different settings. And the more you understand how your own culture, experiences, and biases impact how you see the world, the more open you will be to helping others see the same.

With a little homework and a very open mind, you can improve your cultural IQ and navigate our multicultural landscape with fewer embarrassing gaffes, faux pas, and miscommunications. And you can begin to break down the walls of racism and exclusion.

HOW EMOTIONAL INTELLIGENCE CAN FUEL CULTURAL INTELLIGENCE

We've talked about how Includers can demonstrate cultural intelligence, but cultural intelligence is not a standalone. Western Governors University, an online college, addressed the intersectionality of emotional and cultural intelligence in great leaders in a blog post, writing that truly inclusive leaders also must demonstrate emotional intelligence—empathy toward others.[16] In fact, leaders with emotional intelligence often instinctively know they have to create a work environment in which employees feel like they belong.

What are the "EQ" qualities that "CQ" leaders must demonstrate? WGU cites four in particular:

1. **Self-Awareness.** Our ability to understand our own emotions, biases, and limitations is critical to bridging cultural gaps. Not only that, but self-awareness also sends a powerful signal to others that we value differences in ethnicity, race, gender, religion, and sexual identity and how they affect power dynamics.

2. **Self-Management.** Self-awareness fuels self-management, the ability to manage one's emotions, so we don't make decisions or take actions purely based on how we feel, but rather based on what's in the best interest of the whole. When leaders are in tune with and manage their emotions, they understand how their decisions impact not only them (often as men or white people), but also people of different genders and color and with differing experiences and cultural and religious backgrounds. As WGU notes, "When leaders practice self-management, they are in control of a variety of situations they are placed in."

3. **Social Awareness.** Being in control of one's own emotions and decision-making also gives us the emotional bandwidth to be more in tune with the emotions and feelings of others. The murder of George Floyd marked an emotional watershed for many Black employees who saw themselves in him or his experience. A leader who understands how dynamics and actions impact those around us—who has empathy and awareness—has a powerful advantage when it comes to connecting with employees of color, female partners, and others, which often leads to more inclusive—and responsive—decision-making. A good way for budding Includers to start building social awareness is by reading books like Ibram X. Kendi's *How to Be an Antiracist* or *Caste* by Isabel Wilkerson.

4. **Relationship Management.** A leader's ability to understand and manage their own emotions—and recognize the feelings of others within an organization—heightens their ability to, in a thoughtful way, resolve conflict and diffuse situations that might be fraught with controversy. Addressing racial and gender differences and cross-cultural conflicts starts with an emotionally intelligent leader who models inclusive behavior—listening and learning—to build and manage trusted relationships.

CULTURAL IQ CHECKLIST

What are some specific action items we can take to improve our CQ? Here are seven steps:

1. **Know Your Implicit Biases.** We need to take a long, hard look at ourselves and our social circles and ask, "How might I unintentionally be contributing to the problem?" Are any of my friends of a different culture or religion? How close are they really? If there are any people of color in my neighborhood, are they treated differently than white people? Are their children treated differently—or kept a bit more at a distance? The answers might surprise us.

2. **Understand Your Privilege . . .** Too often, people think "white privilege" means they didn't have a hard life growing up. That's not true—it just means that skin color wasn't one of the things that contributed to those difficulties. When I walk into a room, people make assumptions about where I grew up—in a housing project or, when they hear my Antiguan accent, a tiny shack on an island. Now, a white person may have grown up poor without running water in Appalachia. But when they walk into that same room, nobody makes that assumption.

Your skin color affords you certain privilege in society that you may not even realize.

3. **. . . And Leverage It to Lead by Example.** Privilege also enables us to be advocates—to model the behavior we want to see for our children. Whether it's using our position at work to advocate for building a more diverse team or clearly demonstrating our disapproval if someone uses racist tropes in conversation, becoming an influencer in big ways and small helps create a new normal and inspires those in our circles to follow our lead.

4. **Make the Commitment.** Becoming an Includer starts with our social and professional networks—the groups we get together with on Friday nights or volunteer with at our children's schools. Do these groups include culturally diverse people? Are all the people we work with advancing at the same rate? If the answer to either of these questions is no, then we should be mindful about ways to be inclusive and how we can contribute to making meaningful change. For example, invite someone who is culturally different to socialize at a work event, or better yet, invite them to your home.

5. **Increase Your Interest in Other Cultures.** Notwithstanding America's longstanding history of structural and systemic racism, there are many resources

in our local libraries, communities, and online to help passive sympathizers of all stripes become committed, informed allies and Includers. One resource includes *Waking Up White* by Debby Irving, a white woman from Winchester, Massachusetts, who writes about how, in her forties, a graduate-school class awoke her to the realities of her own unconscious bias. Or look online to see what culturally diverse activities or events are happening in your community or state.

6. **Engage with Culturally Diverse Colleagues or Neighbors.** It's hard to empathize when you haven't really lived in somebody's skin or walked in their shoes—to understand, for instance, the stress factor a Black person confronts every time they walk into a room at work, a store, or a classroom. It's even harder to understand what that would do to everything from our professional advancement to our children's physical health. So sit down with a colleague or a friend and just talk about it for a bit. You'll be amazed with what you might learn.

7. **Prepare to Feel Uncomfortable.** Here's the thing: It's never easy talking about racism. For whites, it feels like guilt or self-flagellation. But for people of color, it can feel like making an excuse—"pulling the race card" when you speak out about getting seated in the back

of the restaurant, or being overlooked at work for an earned promotion. When you start talking about racism, everyone gets nervous and fidgets and squirms. But if racism *didn't* make us uncomfortable, that would be a real problem. If you are uncomfortable speaking about racism as a white person, imagine what it's like for a Black person who has to live with this ugliness every waking day of their life until they die. Ultimately, discomfort is a small price to pay for changes that can create a more racially equitable and just society.

CHAPTER 3

Connections

MIX IT UP AND MULTIPLY

The Rolodex 7

By 2008, I had been running my own PR company for twenty years. I had some big clients and some smaller but equally important ones. I was successful—and part of that was because I had built a diverse network of business, civic, and personal relationships. This was no accident. As a young professional, I had recognized pretty early on that even though I was outgoing and gregarious, Boston was not easy to navigate as a person of color who was also a woman and an immigrant. I involved myself in a number of organizations—serving on the board of nonprofits like the Urban League and engaging the arts community as a member of the Friends of the Boston Ballet and the Museum of Fine Arts Council. In time, these efforts paid off. My parents would've been proud that at every corporate, nonprofit, or political event I attended, the biggest names in town would look at me, say, "Colette!" and come across the room to greet me.

Even still, something gnawed at me: I was almost always one of the few people of color at these events; and over and over, I would see the same other people. There was former Associate Attorney General of the United States Wayne Budd, who at the time was the General Counsel for John Hancock Financial; Marian L. Heard, then President and CEO of United Way of Massachusetts Bay; prominent Boston attorney Fletcher "Flash" Wiley and his wife, Benaree Wiley; and Carol Fulp, who had worked for WCVB, Boston's ABC affiliate. These were impressive, talented, accomplished people, but there were more than just us out there.

Of course, my adopted home was not lacking diverse talent, with 28 percent of residents being foreign-born, 48 percent first-generation immigrants, and 50 percent people of color. So why were there so few people of color at these events? The answer was actually quite simple: because we were the only people of color in the Rolodexes of the event organizers. To me, that said the leaders of these events weren't connected enough to diverse professionals or diverse communities.

Why Connecting Matters

The truth is, your networks are your net worth. They help us make the personal and professional connections necessary to move up in the world, to find new positions, or to access key decision-makers and thought leaders. Networks are formed around shared experiences, and increasingly, with the advent of social media, it is clear that the stronger and more diverse our networks are, the stronger we are as individuals, as leaders, and as organizations.

Perhaps unsurprisingly, stakeholders in the twenty-first century—from customers to shareholders to employees—are increasingly calling for culturally "woke" organizations and executives who know how to cultivate and foster a diverse and inclusive network. By contrast, a lack of trusted, diverse professional or personal associates can undermine confidence in an organization and its leadership. While connections with people whose racial, cultural, and life experiences are different from our own can sometimes be challenging, the benefits are significant.

STAY AWAKE

"Woke" is a term that refers to awareness of social justice and racial justice issues. It is sometimes used in the African American Vernacular English expression "stay woke."

The word "woke" in a political or cultural sense has been used since the mid-twentieth century. Its broad use resurfaced in 2014 in the context of the Black Lives Matter movement as a label for vigilance and activism concerning racial inequalities and other social disparities, such as discrimination against the LGBTQ community, women, immigrants, and other marginalized populations.

Networks, both social and professional, influence the way we think as well as our opportunities. As such, one of the biggest benefits of a diverse network is that it allows us to have a better understanding of cultural sensibilities, social dynamics, and the unique idiosyncrasies that we can apply to business.

Think about it: People of different backgrounds tend to approach problem-solving from a different perspective, and they often bring insights that can be game-changing. Diverse networks also pave the way for new ideas as well as professional and personal relationships. That, in turn, can help with marketing to diverse consumers and supporting an organization's recruitment and engagement of diverse employees.

The results of a diverse network can include new customers, a larger talent pool, better decision-making, and a better reputation. It instantly removes the "we can't find diverse candidates" excuse often used by hiring managers. And it underscores your company's commitment to a diverse workforce and inclusive workplace.

As clear as the benefits of diverse networks are, equally as clear are the drawbacks of not having them. Networks that lack diversity—of thought, background, and ethnicity—can foster discrimination and inequity. They can create an echo chamber of good ideas . . . but also bad ones. And as much as a diverse network can bring people together, a homogeneous one can be exclusionary. And these are real risks for leaders today. It's hard for any of us to envision what happens outside our own networks—out of sight, out of mind, as the saying goes. It's one of the reasons I believe so many white people have a hard time understanding what Black and brown people experience. Why? Because too often they don't have networks that include meaningful social relationships and interactions with people of culturally diverse backgrounds.

How Inclusive Leaders Use Connections to Drive Diversity

Includers Learn from Personal Experience

In my experience, when white people date or marry Black people, they get an up-close-and-personal education on race. Suddenly, they see it firsthand. More than once, I've had white friends with a Black partner tell me, "Wow, this is what Black people go through all the time." And most often it's white men who become the most indignant and become the biggest advocates for racial equality once they actually see the inequality firsthand.

We've seen this dynamic play out in public with relationships such as Alexis Ohanian, the co-founder of Reddit, and tennis star Serena Williams. I saw it for myself with Bill Cohen, a former US senator and Secretary of Defense, and Janet Langhart. In fact, it's a perfect example of why connections matter when it comes to anti-racism. Bill had always been a progressive Republican who believed in equality. While he had marched for civil rights as a young man, when he was elected to Congress, Bill had no people of color on his staff. Then, he married Janet, my best friend and a Black woman who started her career as a model and went on to become a successful television personality. (Some consider her to have been Oprah before Oprah.) When Bill realized how often she'd been passed over and how many opportunities she'd missed, he became her biggest advocate and connected her to those who would see her value. He's argued that she probably could have been as successful as Barbara Walters had it not been for her skin color.

I always say pillow talk can be a powerful opportunity for someone to let their partner know they may not need to follow the status quo. When Bill served as President Clinton's Secretary of Defense, he brought a racial and gender equity lens to his work—a lens that may not have been there prior to his marriage. His staff and the Secret Service agents who protected him were of diverse backgrounds. Very quickly Bill began to understand that Black people may not be able to move up the Pentagon ladder as swiftly as others, so he began looking for diverse candidates he could appoint, promote, or include in his inner circle.

Bill would be the first to tell you that all those decisions came from having a Black wife. Once married, he was able to view the world through Janet's lens, her experiences, her stories, and well-warranted career frustrations. Cohen also has another lens through which to view the world: that of his biracial grandchildren, children of a son from his first marriage who also married a Black woman.

Of course, marrying or dating someone of a different ethnicity or culture is hardly the only way to learn empathy for others or broaden your and their social network. But the point is, the closer diverse relationships are to us—whether it's our friends, neighbors, or those we socialize with—the more likely we are to engage more deeply on issues of equity and inclusion.

Includers Are Intentional About Creating Diverse Networks

Inclusive leaders understand that diverse networks must be a priority for recruiting top talent, generating new thinking, and tapping into new markets. They also recognize that people can be high achievers regardless of race and cultural background. Whether a frontline worker or a CEO, everyone wants to connect and feel they belong. This recognition helps leaders create diverse networks.

When I became frustrated about the dearth of people of color at Boston's social occasions, I decided to go out and start Get Konnected!—a curated series of cross-cultural business and social networking events. Facilitating business and career opportunities for communities of color was no slam dunk, particularly in the middle of the Great Recession. But, I figured, a lot of people were unemployed, and a networking event might be just what they needed.

For my first event, I chose a Tuesday night—the slowest night of the week—to have cocktails in a restaurant. I told the maître d' I could bring one hundred people in on a Tuesday night. He looked me up and down, and I could almost hear him saying, *Right, lady—what kind of people are you going to bring in here?* I continued, "Listen, I know you don't know me, but I have a good reputation in this town. Go online and see that I'm serious."

Then, I spread the word to my network and rang up every former boss and CEO I knew to see if they'd like to stop by. Then I convinced Johnny Diaz, a gay, Latino reporter from the *Boston Globe*, to be there.

Sure enough, we had an enormous turnout in the middle of an economic downturn. There were CEOs, unemployed people, and employed Black, white, Asian, and Latino people. The place was jam-packed—but Johnny was nowhere to be found. I was disappointed, but when I opened the Metro section of the *Boston Globe* the next day, there was a big story highlighting the event and its diversity. It was clear, Johnny had been there. I just hadn't seen him through the crowd.

My company has hosted Get Konnected! events for fifteen years now, bringing together urban and international professionals, business executives, and entrepreneurs from various cultures. For the first seven years, Get Konnected! was free. Now we have corporate partners and charge a nominal fee, dedicated to enriching professional development, forging new business and social relationships, and making Boston a more inclusive city.

Our corporate partners realize that supporting this venture provides a venue where employees of all backgrounds can build diverse and inclusive networks, foster positive cross-cultural relationships, develop their careers, and help make Boston a more welcoming and inclusive city. Get Konnected! also creates specialized lists validating the contributions people from diverse cultural backgrounds are making to the city, the corporate community, and even the global business community.

One of the most important services we provide is the opportunity for leaders to be intentional about diversity. For instance, Dr. Peter Slavin, the former CEO of Massachusetts General Hospital, once chaired a fundraiser for an organization whose events tended to be . . . less than diverse. As a former board member of the hospital, I am part of Peter's network, so he reached out to me and requested I extend an invitation to some of the members of our Get Konnected! network. He was intentional about his desire to host an inclusive and diverse event.

Includers Push Themselves into New Networks

Of course, diverse networking doesn't happen by osmosis. People naturally like to be around folks like themselves. And let's be honest, we don't always like to be challenged, even when we should be. So inclusive leaders need to stretch to move themselves outside of their comfort zones and established networks.

Dave McLaughlin started his career writing screenplays, working in the public sector, and starting companies, one of which was sold to PayPal. Perhaps working in different fields gave him an appreciation for all the benefits different types of networks can bring. Eventually, he landed at WeWork, which provides shared workplaces for start-ups and other companies. Overseeing their US and Canada operations, Dave spent a lot of time thinking about the future of work and how physical workspaces contribute to inclusion—but also exclusion. It wasn't long before he recognized people could benefit from a more intentional focus on diversity and inclusion, and that his own team in Boston could benefit from looking more like the Boston of today.

Dave knew that getting more diverse employees required more diverse referrals, which, in turn, required swimming in more diverse networking pools. So he challenged his team to find diverse candidates, explore diverse networks, and go to places with people different from them. The result was events like Boston's Third Thursday series, a monthly event for Black and Latino professionals and entrepreneurs. These types of initiatives not only gave professionals the opportunity to connect, but also gave WeWork the opportunity to scout for talent.

The results of their efforts were impressive: In 2019, WeWork hosted almost three hundred events focused on Black and Hispanic/Latino professionals and entrepreneurs in Boston. Additionally, the company increased the number of people of color in management positions from one in ten to four in ten, ensuring staff reflected the racial makeup of the city at all levels.

Inclusive leaders don't hope for the best when it comes to fostering diverse networks. They push themselves into new networks, even when it isn't easy. *Especially* when it isn't easy.

Includers Recognize Diversity Doesn't Exclude People

Too often, and for too many people, diversity means Black and brown, but inclusive leaders recognize that's not true diversity. They welcome everyone, and in some cases, insist on their inclusion.

When I started Get Konnected!, I made sure to include and recognize not only people of color for their achievements in diversity, equity, and inclusion, but white people as well. So I did something very on-brand for me, given my reputation for shaking things up: I created an event recognizing white male leaders who were DE&I

allies. I called it "White Men Who Can Jump," inspired by the title of the Wesley Snipes, Woody Harrelson, and Rosie Perez basketball movie.

We honored people like Massachusetts's State Treasurer Steve Grossman, who had made a conscious decision to divest state pension funds from companies that lacked gender and racial diversity on their boards. We also recognized Boston Red Sox owners John Henry and Larry Lucchino for the organization's philanthropic commitment to diversity around the city. Another honoree was Alan Khazei, the co-founder of City Year, one of the models for President Clinton's AmeriCorps program, a domestic Peace Corps designed to lift up rural and urban communities through volunteerism. In all, we have recognized twelve white leaders for their diversity efforts.

When we held our first White Men Who Can Jump event, we were met with a ton of pushback. What I often heard was, "I can't believe that you, Miss Diversity, are doing this!" But my response was straightforward.

"Who occupies the C-suite, the mayor's office, the state treasurer's office, or any of the other places where policy and economic decisions get made? Who controls our health care, academic, and technology institutions?"

Inclusive leaders I know have used employee resource groups (ERGs) to bring together diverse audiences in the workplace, often with a twist. They assign a senior-level manager, many of whom are white, as the executive sponsor of their company's diverse employee networks. Or better yet, they sponsor one of the ERGs themselves, attend the meetings, and keep a close watch on what is reported out.

Tim Sweeney, CEO and President of Liberty Mutual Insurance, took this tack, serving as the executive co-sponsor of Amigos@Liberty, Liberty Mutual's His-panic/Latino ERG, to immerse himself in an environment where he may be in the minority for the first time at the company. Through his work with Amigos@Liberty, as well as Able@Liberty—another ERG, for those with disabilities, caretakers, and allies—and a number of mentoring relationships with Black men and women pro-fessionals at the company, Tim saw an opportunity for inquiry and learning, and in turn, he saw that he needed to be an advocate and ally for inclusion and diversity at the leadership level of the organization. This type of leadership sends a powerful message to the entire orga-nization and its stakeholders that inclusion matters and that culturally diverse and underrepresented employees are important. It also says the organization is committed to creating an inclusive and equitable workplace where everyone feels like they belong.

Includers Accommodate Diverse Networks

One of the most frequently voiced objections to implementing diversity initiatives is, *diversity policies won't work because they are hard to implement and will require businesses to change how they do things*. Well, if diversity is important—whether for employees or new markets—then it's worth changing the business model!

Several years ago, I was consulting with a big bank that wanted to enter New York City's Caribbean market. However, the way they determined the creditworthiness of borrowers was through credit history. That works for a lot of populations, but not for people like those I grew up with. Oh, they had money—often tens of thousands of dollars stashed all around the house—and in most of these homes, just about everybody worked more than one job. But rarely did they have any credit cards, so banks passed them over when they applied for loans to purchase homes.

My suggestion to the client was one that would require the bank to change the way it did business. I said, "What if instead of using traditional credit history, you allowed the use of utility bills and the last six months of rent payments verified by their landlords? That way, you'll know if they are reliable customers, which, at the end of the day, is what you're trying to figure out."

This wasn't rocket science, and with a little massaging, the bank's reluctance softened. The uptake from the Caribbean community was huge.

The bank didn't tell these families—many of whom were newly arrived immigrants with less than five years in the US, or were permanent residents but not yet citizens—*if you want us to work with you, you have to change your cultural norms and habits*. Instead, the bank changed the way it did business to accommodate the borrower, which was seen by the community as a sign of respect. As a result, the bank ended up with a ton of new customers as well as something even more important: loyalty.

Accommodating diverse networks isn't only about moving into new markets. It can also be about doing a better job of connecting in one's own community. Blue Cross Blue Shield of Massachusetts has done just that over the years (see sidebar). Whether it involves leveraging new market opportunities based on changing demographics or building a diverse and inclusive workplace, creating a "new normal" to thrive, survive, and be profitable is going to require new models of doing business—and it's worth it.

DOING BUSINESS WITH A DE&I LENS

In 2021, Blue Cross Blue Shield of Massachusetts announced that it would begin to incentivize doctors who close gaps in care for people of color, incorporating equity measures into its payment models with hospitals and physicians in its network. This wasn't a PR stunt. It was an outgrowth of the diversity, equity, and inclusion strategy forged by its chief executive, Andrew Dreyfus. Its five pillars include:

1. Culture—to achieve an effective and culturally competent organization through an inclusive workforce.

2. Commerce—to deliver the company's products and services to meet its customers' needs through the lens of diversity.

3. Community—to support external partners to address the health and well-being of its diverse community.

4. Careers—to recruit, respect, and retain an inclusive, developed, and diverse workforce.

5. Care—to measure, reduce, and develop interventions to address the inequities in care among its members.[17]

This policy change—and overall strategy—is not simply the right thing to do in the wake of COVID-19 and BLM, it is also fully aligned with Blue Cross Blue Shield's commitment to providing equitable health care to all of its members, and in particular, members of color.

For the health insurer, it was a big change but a simple one. By addressing racial inequities and lowering the cost of care to treat the sickest and most expensive patients, it also makes its own premiums more affordable for everybody. That, as they say, is a win-win.

The Power of Connecting

My own experiences and those of the leaders included in this chapter are only a few ways Includers foster connections with diverse audiences. Inclusive leaders recognize that their leadership is only as strong as the organization they lead and its stakeholders—employees, board members, stockholders, and customers. They also understand that the best ideas don't necessarily come from the top or the bottom, but from within—from robust discussion and debate internally and externally, and at all levels. The secret to making that work is building strong connections within the company and the community.

Cultural Networking Know-How

Networking across cultures can be tricky. As we discussed in the chapter on cultural intelligence, greetings, small talk, eye contact, directness, and self-promotion vary across cultural groups. So when we are embarking on cross-cultural networking, we need to keep a few things in mind, such as:

- **Get Culturally Familiar.** We don't need to read a book before we sit down to network across cultures. But we need to become familiar enough with cultural belief systems. For example, if we're meeting an Asian group of families, it might be helpful to know that in many Asian cultures, elders are highly respected and revered. Age is honor, and by honoring or deferring to elders, we will be considered more respectful in turn.

- **Consider Hierarchy.** Understand how hierarchy works in different cultures. A friend of mine once reminded me that when we go into an event at a Black church, there is often certain seating reserved for different audiences and special guests. So, one tip: In a situation like this, we should follow the guidance of those around us—for example, wait to be seated by an usher because they will know exactly where to place us.

- **Learn Customs.** Understanding something as simple as handshaking and how business cards are exchanged is a network etiquette must. For example, in most Asian cultures, we are expected to read the business card and acknowledge their status and role before putting it in your pocket. And in some cultures, for religious or social reasons, men are not supposed to shake the hand of a woman who is not his wife or daughter. If we're in this situation, we might consider acknowledging the other person's presence without touch.

- **Look and Learn.** Be observant and learn from the behaviors of those in the room. When you walk into a room of people from a different culture, it is often a good idea to take cues from the behavior of those around us. For example, we may be expected to wait to sit down as a sign of respect. This is true of a number of different cultures.

- **Use Your Ears.** Be an active listener to learn what we have in common with others. Try not to

talk too much, and ask questions instead. Here is
our opportunity to really be curious.

- **Mind Your Volume.** Manage our language, tone
and volume, and your nonverbal behavior based
on the environment. For instance, if we speak too
loudly in some cultural settings, we might sound
angry. So modulate our voice, if possible.

- **Respect Personal Space.** In some cultures,
including some Arab cultures, it is normal to get
right up in your personal space to make a point.
Try not to be offended or alarmed by it—it's
not meant as a sign of disrespect but is simply
a cultural norm. So, a good tip is to follow the
example of our host or those familiar with the
particular culture when it comes to intimate
conversations or interactions.

- **Be Flexible.** In most Western cultures, time is
money. But in many developing countries, we
don't make money until we've formed a bond.
Latino and Black audiences often put a premium
on socializing and engaging with one another. So
we shouldn't be too worried about the clock. Go
with the flow.

CHAPTER 4

Communications

MAKE THE MESSAGE MATTER

Listen to the Voices

Growing up in Antigua, my brothers, sisters, and I often listened to the radio. Our parents had a television with a huge antenna on the roof that we had to twist and turn to get programming from the US Virgin Islands. The reception was horrible. So, radio became our media type of choice. As a young girl, I fell in love with radio soap operas. Every weekday afternoon at 12:30 PM, my siblings and I would sit mesmerized by the radio drama *When a Girl Marries*. We also listened to Ephraim John, the Walter Cronkite of Antigua; Dame Yvonne Maginley, the

Barbara Walters of radio; and one of my favorites, a local radio broadcaster and DJ named Joan Samuels. I loved how they all read the news, and I loved the storytelling. I observed how journalists had the opportunity not only to document and photograph what was happening, but also to tell the story authentically as it was happening or had happened. This intrigued me and led to my desire to become a broadcast journalist.

When I arrived in the United States to study broadcast journalism at Boston's Emerson College in the 1970s, I was in for a real culture shock. I was a young woman from a British colony who had attended an all-girls school from the age of nine, where politeness and civility were the tenets of protocol. In other words, when the teacher entered the room, everyone stood up and said good morning, and we only sat down when the teacher signaled us to. So, needless to say, I was shocked when I heard students at Emerson argue, challenge, or even yell at professors, with one even screaming, "You're really pissing me off!" It was an education, to say the least! Now, I was no shrinking violet. In fact, I was quite vocal—I came from a rambunctious family that liked to debate, and as a teenager I even landed a spot on a Saturday morning children's radio show, reading stories for younger kids. But this experience at Emerson opened my eyes to the fact that different people communicate differently.

Why Communications Are Important to Anti-Racism

Huddled next to our radio as a young girl, I had realized how communications have the power to inform, engage, educate, and motivate. Moving to the United States furthered my knowledge of communications and how they have the power to change people's opinions and create connections to diverse audiences. Later, as an immigrant in graduate school, I realized not everyone interprets information the same way, and that how you say something is in some ways as important as what you say. We all bring different lenses to how we view things, and we see things differently based on our culture, gender, faith . . . or even simply the mode or channel by which the information was imparted.

This is particularly important in business today as, according to a Pew Research Center study, major demographic changes are transforming the United States into a more diverse and multicultural nation. And this, in turn, is transforming the US workforce. Having a diverse workforce spanning many cultures and countries presents unique challenges, both within the company itself and with the brand's messaging to the outside world. To meet these challenges, a company needs to be able to communicate effectively to form strong teams, collaborate on the best ideas and practices, and achieve the highest level of success.

Communication can take many forms—in-person meetings, tele-meetings, newsletters, intranet communications, or email, to name a few—and when it comes to diversity, effective communications can help get "buy-in" by ensuring that everyone understands diversity, its importance to the organization, and how to talk about it. And, as I discovered, it also brings people closer to each other.

Some of the benefits of effective communications around diversity include greater awareness of diversity's importance and an increased understanding and mutual appreciation among employees. For customers and other stakeholders, there's a reputational benefit to communicating about the importance of diversity. Today, organizations recognized for diversity, equity, and inclusion best practices and considered "woke" (as in enlightened) are rewarded with greater market share, more brand affiliation, and recognition as an employer of choice. Through effective communications you will inform the public what's important to you and what you're doing about it.

Communicating the importance of inclusion also aligns internal values—what's important to an organization and its leaders—with its external values—what it communicates to outside stakeholders. This in turn shapes how the organization is viewed. The more effective you are in getting this message across, the more likely it is you'll be saying the same thing inside an organization as you do to the public. That way there is no confusion about what an organization says it believes and what it *really* believes when it comes to diversity, equity, and inclusion.

How Inclusive Leaders Use Communications to Drive Diversity

Includers Are Mindful of How They Communicate

We all know that language is very powerful. But individual words are particularly powerful when coming from the leader of an organization. They carry special weight and meaning because what a leader says goes. But, as I've discovered, it's often easy to say things that are intended to mean one thing but actually convey another, particularly when it comes to race.

The Anti-Defamation League has created what they call "Guidelines for Achieving Bias-Free Communication" to help educators avoid racial bias. Includers live by these kinds of rules when they speak or write.

They're aware of words, images, and situations that suggest a group of people are the same—and recognize that no one wants to be defined by their skin color or ethnicity. They also avoid qualifiers that reinforce racial and ethnic stereotypes. Our president, Joe Biden, actually got in trouble with this back in 2008, when he called Barack Obama "bright, clean, and articulate" . . . as if most Black people aren't! Obviously, Obama got over it and made Biden his VP. Well-intended white people often make comments like these when referring to Black people. Sometimes a statement that is meant to compliment can end up being an insult, especially if the speaker isn't aware of the unconscious bias in their words. I once had a client who commented that a status report I sent him was very "professional." What else did he expect?

Includers are mindful to only identify people by race or ethnic origin when it's relevant. A good rule to live by here is, if a communication wouldn't mention someone's race if they were white, it's not worth mentioning if the person is a member of another racial group. Includers tend to avoid terms like "nonwhite" because it conveys that white is the standard. They also give their communications a once-over before speaking to make sure they are not using sayings that have their roots in ethnic slurs. And not just the obvious ones—others like "blackballed," "paddy wagon," or "sold him down the river" all have charged histories.

Mindfulness also means communicating about people of other races or ethnic groups with richness and respect. I was reminded of this when Fletcher "Flash" Wiley became the first Black Board Chair of the Greater Boston Chamber of Commerce in 1994, and the *Boston Globe* ran a photo of him on a basketball court in shorts, a tank top, and high-top sneakers. This was a big deal for one of the oldest chambers in the country, and the publication chose to present him in a way that was not respectful of his achievement. Here again, this was probably unintentional. Wiley was well liked and highly regarded in the business community. But portraying him in this clichéd, unserious way was the type of error that never would've happened with a white person. This is also another argument for diversity in decision-making positions.

Inclusive leaders avoid being patronizing, tokenistic, or clichéd toward any racial or ethnic group. Black history is about more than a single blog piece or a CEO statement. Hispanic Heritage Month can be about family history or politics instead of food and music. Inclusive leaders also periodically check to make sure groups are fairly represented in both internal and external communications like your employee digital newsletter, recruitment and marketing collateral, and advertising. Simple and substantive work when it comes to diversity is *always* better than just checking the box.

THE BENEFITS OF A DIVERSITY, EQUITY, AND INCLUSION COMMUNICATIONS STRATEGY

An effective diversity, equity, and inclusion program is only as good as the comprehensive communications strategy you build around it. Here's why:

1. **Engagement and Education.** It may seem obvious, but communication is critical to engaging and educating people when it comes to diversity, equity, and inclusion. The more you communicate with the full range of your organization's stakeholders—employees and board members, stockholders and community partners, and supply chain partners and customers—the more they will know about its DE&I program and what it seeks to accomplish, and the better they'll understand the importance of diversity, equity, and inclusion and the business and economic imperative for it.

2. **Brand Ambassadors.** Effective communications about diversity, equity, and inclusion can convert stakeholders into DE&I brand ambassadors. And as we know, the more influencers and evangelists we have for DE&I, the more powerful the program is (and the less we have to carry the load all by ourselves).

3. **Safe Spaces.** Communication about diversity, equity, and inclusion also sends a message to employees and staff that their work environment values and welcomes differences. That, in turn, helps to create a culturally safe and inclusive workplace that encourages honest and authentic dialogue.

4. **Momentum.** We have all seen that when the boss tells us to do something, it happens a lot faster than if they stay silent. The same is true of diversity, equity, and inclusion. By communicating from the C-suite level that DE&I is a priority—through an email or a short set of remarks at an internal event—leaders can create momentum for the initiative and underscore the urgency of action.

We often say talk is cheap, but when it comes to diversity, equity, and inclusion, it's essential. If you don't support your diversity strategy with effective communications, you won't get buy-in. You'll create misunderstanding, misinformation, and speculation that can undermine and/or doom the whole program.

Includers Understand the Power of Nonverbal Communication

As powerful as words can be, nonverbal communication can sometimes speak louder.

When I came back to the United States for good as a graduate student, I was a teaching assistant at Emerson for a professor named Ted Hollingworth. He did a lot of work with the Massachusetts State Police, teaching state troopers communications skills and how to treat men and women equally. Over and over, the officers in these trainings insisted they treated everyone the same. To show them this wasn't true, the professor would set up specific interactions and tape them. Then, he would show the tapes and focus on body language and tone. What the tapes revealed was when talking to women, officers leaned in and were accommodating. Hollingsworth showed how the tone and tempo of their voices were modulated. Then, he played a tape of them talking to a man, and pointed out not only their voice quality, but how they stood back and pushed out their chests so their gun was showing. The police officers were shocked! They had no idea their nonverbal communication was letting their bias seep through. The same is true in today's workplace. We may think we treat everyone equally, but our body language often tells a different story. Without even realizing it, we may be more ebullient or outwardly friendly with a white colleague, but more distant or reserved with a person of color.

Inclusive leaders try to be aware of body language and their interactions. They maintain eye contact with people of other cultures (when appropriate) and recognize the importance of modulating their voice. But they also accept that there are going to be some nonverbal cues they simply aren't aware of. So when someone points out an error they've made, they aren't defensive. They see it as a lesson learned and avoid making the same mistake again.

Includers Foster a Culture of Open, Respectful Communication

For diversity to flourish in an organization, individuals need to communicate with one another and learn each other's customs, religions, and cultures. Employees need to know how to talk to one another in a respectful way and see each other's humanity behind their differences. But none of this happens by itself. Includers need to set them up for success.

There's a children's book, by Rosemary Wells, titled *Yoko*. It's about a child who brings a bento box containing sushi to school and is laughed at because of the way the food smells. Eventually, the teacher realizes the girl's feelings are being hurt and has every student bring in a food from their own culture as an exercise to open dialogue and foster learning. Something similar actually happened at the company of one of my clients. A Vietnamese woman was sitting in the cafeteria preparing to enjoy her lunch. When she opened her food container and the aroma emanated, one of her colleagues turned up her nose and stated, "That food smells terrible!" One day, the CEO of the company noticed the Vietnamese woman sitting alone. He asked why she wasn't enjoying lunch with colleagues. She explained, and he was appalled. He sent a letter to his employees discussing the importance of being respectful to colleagues and why their behavior needed to be in keeping with the company's commitment to inclusion. To further show his commitment to diversity, he hosted a series of lunch-and-learns where employees were asked to bring food representative of their culture.

Includers also understand the importance of giving people an opportunity for a do-over to correct their mistakes rather than publicly shaming them. Professor Loretta J. Ross of Smith College talks about how instead of calling people out when they mess up, we should instead call people "in" with respect. For instance, instead of saying that we are "triggered" by an action or statement, she recommends we say we experience "discomfort." She also suggests not publicly shaming people for accidentally misgendering a colleague or for sending a stupid tweet or for something they clearly regret.

Includers don't hope for the best when it comes to respectful communication between employees from varying backgrounds. They set a standard for what they expect—and create settings to facilitate it.

"CALLING IN" CULTURE

As preacher William L. Watkinson once wrote: "It is far better to light the candle than curse the darkness." Over the years, I've documented and celebrated allies who are helping to move the needle on diversity, equity, and inclusion with White Men Who Can Jump and by publishing lists of "woke white women" and the like. Why? Because as my mother used to say, you catch a lot of flies with honey . . . and none with vinegar. It's better to reward people for their good behavior than exert energy calling out their missteps.

So instead of calling out a colleague when they have done or said something that is culturally insensitive or inappropriate, how can Includers "call them in"? Here are some of Professor Ross's ideas, as she shared with the *New York Times*:[18]

1. **Explain How They Can Do Better.** Often, people make mistakes simply because they don't know any better. For instance, many people may still not realize that the term "sexual preference" is not acceptable when discussing gender identity or orientation. Includers don't simply call these people out for being wrong—but help them understand how to get it right the next time.

2. **Take It Offline.** Publicly shaming bad behavior can be useful in egregious circumstances. But Professor

Ross suggests a defter touch can be more effective when discussing a less egregious offense. For instance, Includers may choose instead to send someone a private message over email or Slack, pick up the phone, or walk over to their office for a private conversation rather than calling someone out publicly—which could make them more defensive.

3. **Keep Things in Perspective.** Professor Ross also suggests that the tendency to overstate the harm of an offense is not helpful when we are trying to create a culture of compassion and inclusion. Includers, as leaders, can ensure that the "punishment fits the crime." This isn't about letting someone get away with saying or doing racist or anti-Semitic things, rather that, for a first—and possibly unintentional—offense we encourage empathy, understanding, and learning . . . and make it a teachable moment.

As Professor Ross said, "You're really seeking to hold people accountable for the potential harm that they cause, but you're not going to lose sight of the fact that you're talking to another human being." That's what "calling in" is—and it's what Includers do.

Includers Communicate the Benefits of Diversity and Equity Through Their Work

Inclusive leaders also recognize that helping people understand the benefits of diversity isn't always done through memoranda and press releases—but through their work itself.

I look at leaders like Eric Rosengren, who was President and CEO of the Federal Reserve Bank of Boston. Eric wouldn't describe himself as a particularly dynamic speaker, but he got the importance of communicating diversity and chose to do so through his work. For instance, he made sure his board was diverse, and on his watch, the Boston Fed has created numerous products and studies on the issue of diversity.

One of the most important was the landmark piece called "The Color of Wealth in Boston." The study found that white families in the Boston area have a median net worth of about $250,000—due to the fact that they often own a home and a car and have little credit card debt—while Black households have a median net worth of just $8—because they were less likely to own a home and a car, less likely to work in a highly paid job, and more likely to be in debt.

For all the work people like me—trained communications professionals!—have done to bring attention to inequality and racism, that simple fact—that Black families effectively had only $8 to their name—was what broke the issue through to the mainstream. And it happened because a savvy white man in his fifties from New Jersey (with a South Asian wife, I should add) used his platform to get people's attention.

In short, he let his work communicate the importance of diversity for him and the Boston Fed. And sometimes, that's the most effective communication of all.

Changing the Narrative

Ultimately, discrimination—whether it's based on ethnicity, color, national origin, gender, religion, sexual identity, sexual orientation, or ability—has been with us for centuries. Despite demographic trends moving America toward a more multicultural society, and despite our claims of being an enlightened and evolving society, discrimination has remained with us. In part, this is because our communication and our language have long been used as tools to reinforce bias and shape thought. Includers, including many highlighted in this book, recognize this, and in response, bring the same vigor and obsessive attention to detail to their communications about diversity as they do in letting employees and customers know about the company's key initiatives and business results.

For Includers, communicating consistently and effectively about diversity isn't a "nice" thing to do; it's central to their identity and to their success.

FIVE TIPS FOR INCLUSIVE LANGUAGE

If Includers teach us anything, it's that words matter. So how can we use words to convey tolerance and acceptance? Some important things to keep in mind when speaking or writing to your audience include:

1. **Keep It Relevant.** Only refer to gender, sexual identity, religion, cultural group, or ability when it's relevant to the discussion. If there's no reason to mention that someone is Muslim, then don't.

2. **Avoid Idioms, Jargon, and Acronyms.** Not all abbreviations and slang words are culturally transferrable. Some can exclude those who may not have specialized knowledge of a particular subject and impede effective communication. Others may not translate well from country to country. And still others are rooted in negative connotations and stereotypes. So it's best to avoid using them in culturally diverse situations . . . or at all.

3. **Don't Associate Disabilities with Victimhood . . .** It's no longer culturally acceptable to make jokes about disabilities. But sometimes we still use phrases that can get us in trouble. Includers avoid terms that diminish others' humanity when describing a disability—i.e., "afflicted by," "victim of," or "suffers from."

4. **. . . And Recognize Terms That Describe Real Psychological Disabilities.** Some terms we use to describe people or their behavior are disabilities that people actually possess, like bipolar disorder, OCD, and ADHD. Includers recognize that these should not be metaphors for everyday behaviors and steer clear of derogatory mental health terms such as "schizo" or "psycho."

5. **Be Aware "Guys" Is Not a Gender-Neutral Term.** Using "guys" to mean "people" assumes that the normal, default human being is male. Although "he" and "man" are said to be neutral, studies show these words cause people specifically to think of males. So be mindful when you use them.

THE RIGHT STUFF

While I've explained why we need to use inclusive and culturally appropriate language in different circumstances, it can help to see some examples of what, and what not, to say. It's worth noting that much of this is personal to some, and many of these terms change over the years. As such, readers should be adaptable, and when in doubt, just ask.

Affirmative Terminology	Negative Terminology
People with disabilities	Handicapped, disabled
Person with disability	Impaired, invalid, crippled, afflicted
Person without disability	Normal, healthy, able-bodied
Successful, productive	Courageous, inspirational
Has paraplegia	Paraplegic
Has traumatic brain injury	Is brain damaged
People who are blind or have low vision	The blind
Person with hearing loss	Deaf and dumb
Child who has autism	Autistic child
Has epilepsy	Is epileptic, has fits
Person with intellectual cognitive developmental disability	Retarded, slow, idiot, moron
Person with psychiatric disability or mental illness	Crazy, insane, nuts, psycho
Person of short stature or little person	Dwarf, midget
Has a congenital disability	Has a birth defect
Person who uses a wheelchair	Wheelchair-bound, confined to a wheelchair

CHAPTER 5

Collaboration

ASCEND THROUGH ALLIANCE

Leaders and Legacy

In 2019, I brought together a group of CEOs. Several were peers, some were allies, and the others were founding partners of Get Konnected! It was a crew of White Men Who Could Jump, CEOs from some of the most prestigious hospitals in the world, health insurers, technology leaders, and leaders from workforce development companies. Boston's Mayor Marty Walsh came to kick off the event.

When I took the floor, I asked a simple question: *What do you want your legacy to be?*

All these men were over fifty and weren't going to be in their jobs forever. Each of them stated in one way or another they wanted to move the needle on inclusion. So my goals for the meetings over the next year were simple: increase the senior-level pipeline of diverse talent at each of these CEOs' companies, work to advance more diverse candidates into the C-suite, and advance greater diversity on corporate boards in Boston.

But I also had another goal: I wanted to get these guys together to talk about what they were doing regarding diversity, to see what their peers were doing, and to think about whether they needed to do more. We met once a quarter, and at the end of the year I handed each of them a scorecard I had compiled. These leaders had spent a year meeting with their peers and now it was time to see what had actually happened or changed.

One CEO had hosted a town hall meeting on diversity, equity, and inclusion and unconscious bias with his senior leadership team. Another was instrumental in getting his general counsel, an African American LGBTQ woman, appointed to a corporate board; and another had had all of his direct reports engage in an unconscious bias training, and had set goals for construction companies working to build his company's offices to partner with minority subcontractors. Another CEO hired a Black woman as Executive Vice President and Chief Impact

Officer overseeing all of his company's engagement and philanthropy. Another appointed two C-suite executives to his leadership team: one who was the first person of color to serve as his hospital's Department Chair, and another person of color who became the Vice President of Human Resources. Of course, it wasn't all good news. One CEO lasted only one meeting, but overall there was a lot of progress in a short period of time.

We have seen leaders collaborate along these lines in other contexts. One example I've mentioned before is CEO Action for Diversity & Inclusion, a group started by PricewaterhouseCoopers's Tim Ryan to address the issue of policing. Tim wondered how CEOs could move the needle in the face of a dysfunctional and discriminatory justice system and the effect this system had on their company's Black employees, customers, and communities.

How Inclusive Leaders Use Collaboration to Drive Diversity

Inclusive Leaders Value Collaboration

Inclusion requires more than leadership. It also requires working together to adopt a common goal. Of course, every leader wants to say they have a collaborative culture, but few organizations really do. That's because it's hard work to actually get people working together toward a common goal.

While a diverse workforce offers many benefits, inclusion isn't something you can easily mandate, whether it be for race, age, gender identity, language, political leaning, or sexual orientation. As America becomes more culturally diverse and organizations begin to leverage these seismic demographic changes to create more diverse workforces, challenges still emerge that can inevitably lead to conflict in the workplace.

By contrast, a collaborative culture drives higher employee engagement, better retention, and more innovation. Juliet Bourke and Andrea Espedido Titus wrote in the *Harvard Business Review* that leaders who are effective at collaboration "empower others, pay attention to diversity of thinking and psychological safety, and focus on team cohesion." According to Coqual, formerly the Center for Talent and Innovation, organizations rated highly for diversity and inclusion report 57 percent better collaboration and 19 percent greater staff retention. Researchers also find that employees of these companies are 45 percent more likely to report an improvement on market share over the previous year and are 70 percent more likely to report that their business has captured a new market. So yeah, collaboration is not only the right thing to do; it's also the smart thing to do. But how can leaders become more collaborative?

Includers Develop External Partnerships

Inclusive leaders are collaborators. They get outside of their own bubbles—or as my friend, the author and Harvard Business School professor Rosabeth Moss Kanter, puts it, they "think outside the building."

In a 2020 memo, Wells Fargo CEO Charles W. Scharf blamed the lack of diversity at the bank on "a very limited pool of Black talent to recruit from." When he eventually apologized, he blamed his own unconscious bias. Mr. Scharf may be a very nice man, but his comments showed he was not engaged with any diverse organization outside of his company. Nor was he in touch with what his own company was already doing to fill the pipeline. Across the country, Wells Fargo was already working with Historically Black Colleges and Universities (HBCUs), and here in Boston, the bank had given money to an organization called BUILD Boston, which works with young Black people to build entrepreneurship.

Includers take ownership of external partnerships; they don't just delegate them to someone else. Attending events celebrating these partnerships sends the message to people of color that this is an organization that wants to do business with someone like them. And believe me, people respond. I once had a C-suite executive tell me, "I want you to coach me." He had just returned from an event where another CEO was received like a celebrity. Additionally, he said, "When I go to minority events, I'm the one in the minority, and no one can vouch for me except for my wife and the two staffers I brought with me." This wasn't a position he wanted to be in. He was the president of a division in a global company and recognized he needed to be able to walk into a room at one of these events, know at least a third of the people, and be comfortable walking up and introducing himself to the other two-thirds.

His experience shows that collaboration is more than just working together. One thing I've noticed that can often spur collaboration within a company is competitiveness. When trying to drive change in the corridors of power, it's good to remember that the only people more competitive than white males are white male CEOs.

Nobody wants to be left behind. I noted this when I sent out the first draft of the progress report to the group of enlightened Boston executives I now called CEO Konnection! Once they all saw which people had outperformed the group and what they had done, the rest started talking to their own internal diversity people to see what they had done that year. None of them wanted a competitor to outshine them. That showed me you can use competition to inspire collaboration. Within the framework, we had competitive companies realizing they could learn from each other and leverage best practices.

The benefits of external collaboration on diversity issues can create a virtuous cycle. Strengthening ties with civic and professional affinity groups that have good relationships with diverse populations is a good way to build equity and a strong reputation as a good corporate citizen—but it also creates a halo effect internally and amplifies the commitment to current employees of color. These relationships, focused on diversity issues, also give employees a sense of pride about working for a company that appreciates all people. Inclusive leaders never underestimate the impact of a diversity-positive reputation, how it will attract new culturally diverse employees, and how it will help keep them.

Includers Insist on Shared Accountability and Visible Participation

Of course, the real mark of an organization's leader is the effect they have on the organization itself. Inclusive leaders not only excel at collaboration, but they also build a culture of collaboration among the people around them, making sure it's expected and nurtured. This is critical to creating an inclusive organization, because by definition, collaboration requires inclusion.

So where do you start? True collaboration can't be a top-down effort. For it to work, you need shared accountability and responsibility. Everybody has to do their part, from front-line staff to senior management. Some examples include mandatory diversity and implicit bias training for all employees, including leadership. These are key to helping employees learn about the benefits of equity and inclusion and how to respect their colleagues. In the era of the #MeToo, Black Lives Matter, and LGBTQ rights movements, relationships at work across race, gender, and other dimensions of difference take on heightened importance. These relationships also encourage employees to be tolerant, respectful, and accepting of differences and to value and support the opinions and ideas of others.

Visible participation is another way of exhibiting accountability. After all, Charles Scharf was right about one thing: He *did* have unconscious bias when he said there weren't enough Black people in the pipeline. He didn't realize there were people within his own company. So, we need to make sure we as leaders not only participate in trainings but do so along with everyone else, rather than in a special session. In other words, be seen. It sends a powerful message.

Sponsorship of diversity initiatives in which the CEO and senior leadership are actively engaged is another form of active and visible collaboration.

Includers Identify and Overcome Obstacles to Collaboration

Perhaps it goes without saying that to collaborate effectively you need to know what obstacles are in your way. Within organizations, departments tend to work in silos, which fosters separation and keeps employees distanced from one another. On the other hand, a diverse, unique, and collaborative staff strengthens company culture.

One way to overcome the silo effect is to develop cross-functional projects and events such as interactive lunch exchange programs between departments, C-suite roundtables or fireside chats with thought leaders and experts, and internal networking events. These events don't necessarily have to be diversity-focused. They can be peer-to-peer interactions that create an inclusive and collaborative work environment and allow employees to connect with each other, meet new coworkers, and learn from and about each other. This ultimately strengthens a sense of belonging and inclusion.

Mentorship and sponsorship can also be critical to collaborative efforts. Corporations such as American Express and Bank of America have created programs that accelerate the progress of women and people of color by pairing them with more experienced senior leaders—or someone who simply knows the organization well—who help them learn the ropes and advocate for them, not just in their first weeks or months on the job, but over the long haul.

Even still, mentorship advice alone is not always enough to overcome barriers to diversity. A sponsor's meaningful advocacy can make all the difference in advancing one's career. As the *Harvard Business Review* says, "Sponsorship expands that person's visibility within the organization, models self-advancing behavior, and directly involves the protégé in experiences that will provide opportunities for career advancement." This can be done by putting their name forward for a promotion or meeting invite or advocating for their work when they are not in the room. As the *HBR* says, "The sponsor puts their professional reputation and branding behind the protégé."[19]

Research has shown that women of color who say they have sponsors are 81 percent more likely to be satisfied with their career progression than those without sponsors. A good example of how this approach can impact diverse advancement is Wayland Hicks's mentorship and sponsorship of Ursula Burns at Xerox, which we discussed in our chapter on character.

Of course, people can be obstacles, too. Sometimes companies and organizations spend a lot of time either placating people who are contrarians or finding ways to work around them. So it can be important to identify employees who are resistant to collaboration, and if necessary, remove them from the equation.

My company experienced such a situation with a Get Konnected! CEO Konnection! event. At the outset, a participating business leader maintained he was fully on board with our mission. This was someone whose company had offices in Africa, Asia, and the Middle East, and had any number of reasons for improving his company's diversity posture. But despite insisting he was a progressive CEO, it became clear almost immediately that he wasn't invested in this collaboration. He was argumentative. His board wasn't diverse, and unlike others, he was defensive about it. He went so far as to diminish the progress of others when they spoke about how they were diversifying their companies. Ultimately, this CEO had a different perception of diversity, and there was no changing his mind.

In my experience, people either need to step up or step out. If you are reading this book, you have an interest in understanding diversity and why it's an asset to your business. But that's not everyone's stance. If you have to work to convince a senior executive in today's environment that having women and people of color in their employ as part of their leadership and on their boards is good for business, they don't see the value of diversity—and probably never will.

Inclusive leaders don't let this kind of thing drag down their DE&I efforts. So if someone is not on board with inclusion, then send a clear message you aren't on board with them—and that this may not be the organization they should be working with.

Includers Encourage Collaboration by Valuing and Celebrating Employee Differences

One of the most important ways to create enthusiastic collaborators is to demonstrate to employees that you respect and value their backgrounds and traditions and invite them to share them in the workplace.

A good example is Vertex Pharmaceuticals. The company holds an annual Inclusion, Diversity, and Equity Week to celebrate the multiple nationalities and cultural diversity of its employees in the US and abroad. The week features a series of events, employee and guest speakers, and foods from employees' home countries.

It's not all about forcing people into the same room together; it's also about giving people space to be themselves. Some companies offer meditation or prayer rooms, or what some refer to as "wellness rooms." Buffalo, New York–based manufacturer of mobile computers Bak USA created a reflection space where Muslim employees could pray. In the same vein, Salesforce, Google, Yahoo, Nike, Pearson, and HBO have all designated official meditation spaces in their corporate offices. These efforts allow companies to show respect for differences—which can make collaboration across the organization easier in the long run.

Celebrating employee differences may seem trivial. But doing so sends two messages to everyone, both inside and outside of the company: Diverse employees are valued by the company, and the same is expected of colleagues and vendors.

Includers Facilitate and Incentivize Collaboration

One of the best ways to build a more collaborative culture is to solicit employee input. Too often, leaders think it's solely their responsibility to solve their company's problems. After all, they've been hired to lead.

But why not ask people what they think? Soliciting employee input to overcome challenges allows them to take ownership, which is essential for inclusion to work. Getting their feedback is a way to let them be heard, to empower them, and to let them know that their input, ideas, and recommendations matter.

According to the Society for Human Resource Management, 70 percent of employees rank being empowered to take action at work when a problem or opportunity arises as having a critical impact on their engagement.[20] There are various ways to solicit employee opinions, motivations, and sentiments: traditional online surveys, video conferencing, town hall meetings, and one-on-one meetings, to name a few. But not surprisingly, employees often offer the best solutions to workforce challenges during collaboration.

Employee resource groups—or ERGs—are a great way to engage, empower, and elevate your employees. They give people an opportunity to come together as well as meet colleagues from other departments, have a voice, and support an organization's diversity initiatives.

Participating in an ERG allows employees to collaborate with their teammates and coworkers to plan events, build mentee-mentor relationships, and interact with senior management through the group's executive sponsors. ERGs can also be leveraged to support a company's corporate social responsibility and philanthropic efforts through volunteering in a community and mentoring underserved youth. These also foster collaboration and teamwork.

Giving employees an opportunity to "show their stuff"—along with the knowledge that executives want to hear their best ideas because they know it can improve the bottom line—gives them a powerful incentive to come to the table.

The Power of Working Together

Becoming a collaborative leader doesn't just happen, and let's face it, most executives are not accustomed to ceding control to others to achieve a common goal. Further, as Bourke and Titus wrote in the *Harvard Business Review*, "Inclusive leadership is not about occasional grand gestures, but regular, smaller-scale comments and actions."[21] With a little practice, and some work, you can show how you are building a culture of collaboration in your organization to include more people in decision-making and send the message that you are serious about being a collaborative leader. The payoff will be enormous.

STEPS TO COLLABORATION SUCCESS

1. **Develop Cross-Functional Projects and Events.** There is no better way to make diversity, equity, and inclusion integral to a company's bottom line than bringing people together from different parts of the organization. Whether it's through brown bag lunches or a virtual

fireside chat with thought leaders and experts over Zoom, create opportunities for employees to connect, discuss, and debate issues outside of their usual job descriptions.

2. **Be Visible in Your Participation.** Collaboration isn't just for employees. Leaders who show they are collaborators are more likely to be supported by their staff through good times and bad. So encourage your entire C-suite and leadership team to participate in diversity trainings, mentorships, and sponsorships in meaningful ways.

3. **Promote Mentorship and Sponsorships.** Having mentors and sponsors that promote advancement throughout an organization is key to fostering collaboration. Executives who are serious about recruiting and retaining diverse talent should look to The Mentor Method, an enterprise platform that helps companies keep and develop diverse talent through mentorship. Janice Omadeke, its CEO and founder, was a subject matter expert at President Obama's 2016 White House summit to build the technology workforce of the future.

4. **Forge External Partnerships.** Get outside of your bubble and seek out mutually beneficial partnerships with credible companies and organizations. Choose from civic, service, education, and professional organizations

that have strong ties and good relationships with diverse communities. And support equitable corporate philanthropy.

5. **Don't Waste Time with "Diversity Trolls."** Collaboration is not all about creating new programs or events. Use your own judgment about how people work together. If someone continues to throw obstacles in the way that make it hard for a group of employees to move forward with diversity, equity, and inclusion, don't waste time appeasing them. Be decisive.

CHAPTER 6

Courage

FEARLESS LEADERSHIP, FOCUSED DECISIONS

White Men Opened the Door

In 1985, I was working for Royal Sonesta Hotel, head-quartered in Cambridge, Massachusetts, when I realized I was ready to start my own business. So, I told my boss, Paul Sonnabend, I wanted to launch my own PR business. And then I told him I wanted Sonesta to be my first client. I had a few expectations as I made this bold statement . . . being fired was one of them. I also knew that if he said yes to becoming a client, that check would be less than my current salary. But I was willing to take a chance on both. If I was fired, well, I was leaving anyway; and if the hotel became a client, it would serve as a springboard to other businesses.

What I wasn't expecting was what he offered me: the opportunity to use my old office three days a week for my new business and to keep me on the company's health insurance plan even though I was now a consultant rather than an employee. I was amazed, pleasantly surprised, and deeply touched by his generosity and demonstration of support.

Around the same time, I reached out to Bob Spiller, the CEO of Boston Five Cents Savings Bank. I knew Bob from a previous job, and I ostensibly called him to talk about his TV ads. Five Cents Savings Bank was the only bank in Boston with a branch in Roxbury, one of the city's minority neighborhoods. Five Cents also had Black members on their advisory board, something virtually no one else had back then. The problem? They hadn't leveraged any of it.

During our call, I told Bob his ads were wonderful, but that they didn't tell the full story because there were no people of color in them. I explained his bank was leaving money on the table and sending the wrong message—that Five Cents didn't want the business of Black people. I knew that wasn't true. After all, they wouldn't be in the heart of the Black community if they didn't want the residents' and business owners' business.

Based on that conversation, Bob hired me as a consultant on ethnic marketing. I reviewed the bank's collateral
materials and incorporated Black and brown faces into
them. I also advised him to cohost a series on first-time
home buying in Roxbury along with the Twelfth Baptist
Church. Bob and others at the bank were skeptical, won-
dering if I could get anyone to attend, but they moved
forward with the plan. As they say in *Field of Dreams*,
"If you build it, they will come." And sure enough, 150
people showed up.

Later, I partnered Boston Five Cents Savings Bank
with Roxbury Community College. The bank hired their
students as part-time tellers and gave them opportunities to move up the ladder.

Around the same time, community activists and
the Lawyers' Committee for Civil Rights Under Law
were starting to target banks for the practice of redlin-
ing, which prevents certain people—usually people of
color—from receiving loans or purchasing homes in certain neighborhoods. Most banks were fearful of receiving negative press and reputational damage from their
participation in this type of illegal activity. I told Bob,
"You have nothing to worry about. You *are* lending in
these communities!" He heard me, and we put together
a presentation highlighting what Five Cents Savings
Bank was doing in the Black community. After the

presentation, one of the activists asked me to present Boston Five Cents Savings Bank's model to other banks in Boston as encouragement to follow suit.

Why am I sharing these stories? Because they tell us a lot about courage. Certainly, I had my own share—perhaps even a bit of arrogance. Imagine quitting your job to start your own business and asking your boss to become your first client! But as a Black woman in Boston trying to start my own business, that's what was necessary—especially back then.

But it isn't my own courage that was notable. It was Paul's, and it was Bob's. It took courage to support an employee going into a new venture, and it took courage for a profitable bank to go after a market in a more aggressive manner. It took courage for the bank to partner with a Black Realtor, who knew the clientele and the historic faith-based Twelfth Baptist Church.

The courage of these Includers provided Black people with an alternative to predatory payday lenders. Their companies were able to show they were deeply engaged in the community, partnering with trusted institutions and helping people build wealth. The civil rights group had a model they could bring to other banks. And because of their courage, I got the wins needed to grow as a young Black entrepreneur.

When someone has the courage to facilitate access and opportunity for those who are underrepresented and/or marginalized, it can have a profound impact on careers, people, and business.

Why Courage Is Critical to Anti-Racism

President Franklin D. Roosevelt is quoted as having said, *"Courage is not the absence of fear, but rather the assessment that something else is more important than fear."* I like this definition as it relates to race and racial equity because they are two of the most feared subjects in America. They make people extraordinarily uncomfortable, but through courage, we can recognize their importance and fight for equity despite our discomfort.

In the aftermath of George Floyd's murder and its traumatizing effect on the nation, we have witnessed many clear examples of courageous leadership across industries. University presidents and state governors stepped up efforts to remove Confederate monuments and flags from their institutions and state buildings. CEOs and academic leaders held conversations on race and racial inequity with their employees, faculty, and students, and made major financial commitments to address structural and systemic racism. All showed courage by raising their voices on social issues that will impact not only their employees and students of color but also society as a whole. Racial equity was assessed to be more important than fear.

On the journey to end structural and systemic racism and inequality, it's important to recognize courage as one of the single most important qualities of an inclusive leader. It fuels passion to stand up and speak out whenever and wherever there is inequity and injustice. It also provides the fortitude to place oneself in the uncomfortable position of coming to the aid of others who are aren't necessarily a priority for our culture and society.

Being courageous can be even more difficult when it comes to addressing the structural and systemic racism or gender inequality that is so much a part of American culture. For an example of this, we can look at people like the late Congressman John Lewis, who at any point during his civil rights journey could have been killed, and almost was.

But courage isn't only about being a civil rights leader. I mentioned earlier in this book that Prince Harry's character was one reason he followed his heart and married a divorced Black woman instead of caving to the expectations of society and his family. But it was his courage that led him to give up the life of a royal to protect his wife and child from the racism expressed in the press and within their own home.

How Includers Are Courageous in the Face of Racism

Not everyone has choices that are quite so clear as Prince Harry's, but everyone can be courageous in the face of racism or inequity, and that courage can actually produce results.

Includers Speak Out Against Racism

To begin with, inclusive leaders don't stay silent in the face of racism or discrimination.

Doug Conant, former CEO of the Campbell Soup Company and Chairman of the Kellogg Executive Leadership Institute at Northwestern University, has spoken powerfully on the subject of courage. He wrote, "I believe that when a CEO visibly stands for openness, diversity, and inclusion, it sends an essential message to the organization."[22] He went on to say he "began every staff and global leadership meeting with the topics of diversity and inclusion" because he had realized the Campbell Soup Company workforce lacked the diversity of the people they were serving.

In 2016, Deloitte Australia reported the findings of a study that identified six signature traits of inclusive leaders. Drawing from the experience of subject-matter experts and best-in-class leaders in diverse sectors across the world, the study identified courage as one of these signature traits. A highly inclusive leader is committed to lead with courage by speaking up and challenging the status quo while also recognizing their personal limitations.

Courageous leaders are never quiet or reticent about discussing the challenging topics of diversity, racial equity, and inclusion. Inclusive, savvy leaders choose courage over comfort, and they understand it is not up to those who are the victims of racism to curate the conversation. As Mellody Hobson, a Black woman and President and co-CEO of Ariel Investments said in a powerful TED Talk, we need to "move from being color blind to being color brave,"[23] and to speak boldly and courageously about race—particularly about diversity in hiring, as it makes for better business and a better society. Indeed, it is the role of the leader to start the conversation and draw it to its natural conclusion.

Includers Initiate and Lead Tough Conversations

Racism isn't an easy topic to discuss. It may even make you queasy. But part of being courageous is getting out of your comfort zone. Leaders can facilitate that.

In 1971, CBS began airing Norman Lear's sitcom *All in the Family*, a show that exposed the stupidity of racial prejudice by making us laugh at it and at the show's protagonist, Archie Bunker. Typically, the show would include Archie blustering about Black people; about his wife, Edith; or about his Polish son-in-law, Michael, who he often referred to as "meathead" or "dumb Polack." Importantly, however, Archie almost never had the last laugh. Nearly every episode ended with Archie getting the rug pulled out from under him, perhaps most famously when Sammy Davis Jr., a Black entertainer he loved and used as an example to deny he was racist, appeared on the show and planted a big kiss on his cheek.

The show didn't provide a solution to racism. What TV show could? And Lear himself, despite his liberal politics, did not have a diverse staff writing and directing his myriad shows in the 1970s. But *All in the Family* started an important conversation in the wake of the Civil Rights Movement about the ugly ignorance of racism as well as the casual ways it was perpetuated and deeply embedded in our society.

Inclusive leaders have the courage—but also the power—to start these hard but important conversations. For instance, Bank of America is a financial behemoth—the kind of company we don't think of as fully understanding race relations. But in 2015, the bank opened the door to what they called "courageous conversations," a program featuring dialogues ranging from small conversations within teams or employee networks to enterprise-wise conversations with community partners. Topics include everything from race, gender dynamics, and LGBTQ equality to the role of the white community in diversity, social justice, and inclusion in the workplace. Moreover, the bank connected the program to local and national current events, hosting panels in the wake of violence in Dallas, Baton Rouge, Minneapolis, and Charlotte. To date, the program has reached over sixty thousand employees, including the bank's Board of Directors, global senior leaders, and local market presidents.

Blue Cross Blue Shield has also had the courage to tackle tough conversations. Stephanie Browne, the company's Vice President of Talent Acquisition and Chief Diversity, Equity, and Inclusion Officer in Massachusetts, engaged and encouraged her employee resource groups to facilitate dialogue. Since the killing of George Floyd, the company's Black Professional Network has focused on building a library of best practices to talk about race with peers, children, and leaders. It has also hosted biweekly dialogues and held learning sessions with other employees.

Conversations such as these send the message that a company welcomes dialogue on issues important to them and to the communities they serve. It's not easy to have these discussions, but they can play a big role in creating understanding and respect for differences.

Includers Make Courageous Investments

Following George Floyd's killing and the subsequent protests, countless companies wrote checks to support anti-racism. While most were well-intentioned, some were smarter and more courageous than others. Netflix, for example, invested $100 million, 2 percent of its cash holdings, in Black-owned banks serving low-income neighborhoods. They dedicated $25 million to Local Initiatives Support Corporation, a development finance company with thirty-eight offices across the country that backs Black entrepreneurs across a variety of businesses. And they gave $5 million to the Black Lives Matter Global Network Foundation, which was organizing protests around the country.

But that's not all. Netflix's co-founder, Chairman, and co-CEO Reed Hastings and his wife, Patricia Ann Quillin, gave a startling $120 million to HBCUs and $1 million to support police reform. While, in some ways, these were small investments for very large companies and wealthy people, it was estimated by Netflix that if every company in the S&P 500 allocated a similarly modest amount of their cash holdings into efforts such as the

GK Fund, the New Commonwealth Fund, and the Black
Economic Development Fund, each percent of their cash
would represent $20–$30 billion of new capital.[24] Leading that effort for Netflix was Aaron Mitchell, at the time
the company's Director of Talent Acquisition. Inspired by
*The Color of Money: Black Banks and the Racial Wealth
Gap* by Mehrsa Baradaran, Mitchell had the savvy and
smarts to recognize that these were not only investments
in Black communities—but also in Netflix's own ability
to attract talent.

Making these investments is good stuff. But doing so
before a crisis is truly courageous. Long before America's
2020 racial awakening, Bob Rivers, Chairman and CEO
of Eastern Bank, was frustrated that Black and brown
companies struggled to scale and grow in Boston. Despite
the rhetoric he heard from the business community,
he knew the real reason: Most of these businesses were
undercapitalized. They simply didn't have enough access
to capital to grow at the same level as white-owned businesses. So, Bob took the courageous leap of starting the
Foundation for Business Equity to help invest in Black
and brown companies. He also put companies (including
mine) through a program that made recommendations
for growth and put their leaders in touch with resources
they didn't otherwise have access to. Then, he set up an
integrated ecosystem to help drive the scaling of Black

and brown businesses, not only to create more wealth for key principals, but also to create more jobs in communities that really need them.

Backing one's rhetoric with wealth is a critical and courageous way to show that inclusion matters while also impacting marginalized communities in ways big and small.

Includers Are Courageous in Acknowledging Their Own Ignorance

Inclusive leaders also recognize that showing vulnerability is one of the best ways to convey the urgency and systemic and insidious nature of racism. Earlier in this book, I described how leaders use this vulnerability to demonstrate cultural IQ and to connect with diverse audiences. But this quality is not merely transactional.

Not long after the national protests began in 2020, Bob Rivers told me about conversations he had with members of the Black community about how the George Floyd, Breonna Taylor, and Ahmaud Arbery killings had impacted them. This proven Includer, anti-racism accomplice, and White Man Who *Can* Jump told me that as much as he's done on inclusion, he still didn't understand the level of pain that these incidents and others have inflicted. In describing the deep feelings triggered in Black people in the wake of Breonna Taylor being killed in her own home, Bob said, "I felt humbled by and ashamed by how little I actually knew."

Conveying an awareness of your own ignorance sends a powerful message about how much work will be required to really begin to change more than four hundred years of structural racism. It also draws attention to the impact each of us can make as an individual on a problem that can seem so overwhelming. And it reminds us that while none of us can boil the ocean, we aren't powerless. Through courageous, reflective actions we can take small steps with really big implications that lead to really big outcomes.

Showing Courage in the Face of Uncertainty

Some of us are more naturally courageous than others. While some of us are confident, others tend to be more conservative and risk averse. But to be an inclusive leader, you must shed those doubts and old ways of working. You must be comfortable with being vulnerable and not having all the answers.

Being an Includer requires finding our courage to look deeply inside ourselves and take actions that make us, and those around us, uncomfortable. It's not easy, but on the road to becoming an anti-racism accomplice, it is a must.

FOUR WAYS LEADERS CAN SHOW COURAGE

CEOs of some of our largest companies with vision, talent, and resources are in a unique position to take courageous action, without being constrained or cajoled by the government. Some ways CEOs can show courage to advance racial equity include:

1. **Advocate for Better Education.** Business leaders should financially support and be the chief advocates for better primary and secondary education. With 10 percent of our population functionally illiterate, coupled with the shortage of skilled labor, education in the twenty-first century must become both a corporate and government imperative.

2. **Forge Strong Ties with Minority CEOs.** CEOs are by nature social animals. White business leaders can show courage by partnering or even building social relationships with the CEOs of businesses owned by people of color. Interaction can be done in mutually comfortable settings from the golf course to the dinner

table, as well as through various communications channels from emails to FaceTime.

3. **Be Proactive About Philanthropy.** An "easy win" for Includers is to engage in philanthropy that is responsive to the challenges facing a diverse society and the changing business environment. Corporate giving can no longer be done ad hoc. Proactive and venture philanthropy can manage change as well as differentiate a company from its competitors.

4. **Lobby Government on Behalf of Diverse Communities.** Business leaders operate in rarefied air when it comes to regulators and policymakers. Whether it is lobbying the government for creative, urban-focused business incentives (such as tax offsets that encourage the development and expansion of small and mid-sized minority-owned businesses), supporting alternative transportation that allows urban residents to take advantage of suburban employment opportunities, or pushing for affordable housing, using the power of lobbying to advocate for non-business interests sends a strong signal about the type of courageous leadership an organization has.

CHAPTER 7

Commitment

STAY THE COURSE AND WIN

Persistence Pays Off

Over the course of this book, I've shared examples of what inclusive leadership looks like, the qualities these leaders share, and the different ways they approach the often-thorny issues of discrimination and racism. To be sure, not every inclusive leader follows the same path. Some, like Bob Rivers, Mitch Landrieu, or Justin Trudeau, are bolder and more outspoken. Others choose small, consistent gestures and prefer to lead by example. Some naturally have a high cultural IQ, and others must work at learning the rules of the road when it comes to things like understanding that some cultures put social connection ahead of business—that you must break bread before diving into business—or asking questions before talking about yourself. While there are some commonalities, it all depends on the leader, their personality, and the situation they face.

But there is one quality all truly inclusive leaders embrace without hesitation, and that's commitment to diversity and inclusion. Includers take action, committing themselves and their organizations to inclusion. They recognize talk is cheap and what you actually do is what ultimately matters.

So, how do Includers commit to inclusion? What does that look like? Here again, there are multiple ways to skin this cat, but at the end of the day, there are a few essential ways that every leader and organization should consider, many of which are low-hanging fruit.

How Inclusive Leaders Use Commitment to Drive Diversity

Includers Put Diversity in the C-Suite

Inclusive leadership recognizes change has to start at the top. This isn't something that is up for debate. Your company can't say it cares about diversity and inclusion and

have a white, male CEO and an all-white board of directors advising your CEO.

Earlier in this book, I discussed how Tom Bartlett of
American Tower recognized that to be a truly inclusive
leader he needed to let his employees know he was inter-
ested in their perspectives on where his company had
gaps. As a result of the diversity audit he requested, he
decided to create a full-time Chief Diversity Officer position at his company. This is step one to getting it right as
an Includer.

The person hired for this position should have a broad
mandate and be empowered to launch a company-wide
equity initiative that ties all business performance to
how well it incorporates diversity, equity, and inclusion.
This position should not be buried in human resources,
but should report directly to the CEO.

The next best step is a diversity, equity, and inclusion
committee on the board itself. This group should meet
on a regular basis and interact with the Chief Diversity
Officer.

Includers Prioritize Supplier Diversity

In 2020, my company created the GK! Market, Boston
and Massachusetts's first online, B2B/B2C culturally
diverse procurement database. It was designed as a platform to help corporations develop an inclusive approach

to strengthen their commitment to their supplier diversity program and close the wealth gap, and to make it easy for companies to search and find BIPOC-, women-, veteran-, and LGBTQ-owned businesses by the services they provide.

Small businesses, particularly those with Black and brown owners, were severely impacted by two pandemics: COVID-19 and racial inequity. This free service provides these small businesses in the Greater Boston area the opportunity to promote their goods and services on a digital platform where they may engage with consumers and those wanting to support them.

I've talked about the racial wealth gap, and one of its primary victims is Black- and brown-owned businesses. A big step toward closing the racial wealth gap starts with giving businesses owned by people of color access and opportunity. Wayne Budd did just that. After serving as Associate Attorney General under President George H. W. Bush, Wayne later became general counsel of John Hancock Financial, where he instructed his procurement team to identify Tier 1 vendors, including attorneys, law firms, and accounting firms, to outsource portions of John Hancock's work to businesses owned by people of color. This wasn't a matter of ideology, but good business, and the results were impressive.

When businesses wake up to this issue, BIPOC entrepreneurs get access and opportunity for their businesses. And companies that spend millions of dollars on procurement get more efficiency and a greater potential for cost savings—as study after study shows supplier diversity often results in less nepotism and less cronyism. Everyone wins!

Addressing diversity and inclusion at the vendor level can also produce quick results. At a time when companies across the board are enhancing their diversity efforts, supplier diversity can open an important door to changing corporate culture more broadly.

As part of their commitment, inclusive leaders are smart to establish a supplier diversity program with ambitious targets—say, 20 percent—that is reported to the CEO on a quarterly basis. Tangible monetary targets for purchasing goods and services demonstrate that companies doing business with small minority- and women-owned businesses generate a multiplier effect; not only do they benefit these companies, but they also allow these businesses in turn to hire more people of color.

Increasing supplier diversity—like hiring a chief diversity officer and creating a board DE&I committee—is one of the best and easiest ways to make an impact.

Includers Tie Compensation to Diversity and Inclusion

As the saying goes, "Money talks, BS walks." Inclusive leaders understand this. They know that you can do everything I've discussed on these pages—start courageous conversations; improve a company's cultural intelligence; communicate regularly about the importance of diversity, equity, and inclusion; show character; communicate, and commit . . . but one thing thirty years in business has taught me is that you will never get there on these issues unless people's compensation is at stake.

When Wayne Budd charged John Hancock Financial with identifying diverse firms as legal subcontractors, he didn't stop there. Since having diverse suppliers wasn't a nicety but a must, he tied their contract renewal to how successful they were in finding and subcontracting legal work to culturally diverse law firms.

In 2021, Andrew Dreyfus, the CEO of Blue Cross Blue Shield Massachusetts, announced that the health insurer would begin paying doctors more for closing gaps in care. By bringing a racial equity and cultural competence lens to their practice, BCBS incentivizes doctors who might otherwise not focus on the differences between how white patients and Black and brown patients are cared for.

Executives across the spectrum can do this with their providers, clients, and vendors as well—and it creates a multiplier effect. In my experience, I've learned when you make an initiative part of someone's review and finances, people get committed to that initiative real fast.

Includers Commit to Tapping into Culturally Diverse Markets

I've also discussed how companies' expansion into diverse markets benefits both the communities and the companies. Where many leaders see the risks of wading into a market with which they are unfamiliar, Includers recognize that when they exclude culturally diverse markets, they are literally leaving money on the table.

When a Shaw's supermarket was opening in Rhode Island, the chain's leadership knew they had to accommodate the state's growing Latino population. For many Latino consumers, grocery shopping is more than a chore. It is often a social activity as well. For Shaw's, that meant more than bilingual signage—it also meant creating a floorplan with wider aisles to accommodate carts and shoppers parked side-by-side for conversation.

Another example is the Mass General Brigham hospital system, which found that during the COVID-19 pandemic, thousands of patients with the greatest needs couldn't navigate their patient portal to receive care and didn't speak English. As a result, its CEO, Anne Klibanski, created a new permanent workforce fluent in a dozen languages spoken in the Boston area, including Portuguese, Cantonese, and Cape Verdean Creole. That not only benefits the patients, but also gives Mass General Brigham—whose goal is to become a more "patient-centered health care system"—the ability to communicate with a wider variety of culturally diverse patients.

Opening a new store, chapter, or franchise in a diverse market—or translating your business into multiple languages spoken by your customers—is a great way to expand the diversity of not only your customers, but your employee base as well. Employing people who look like and speak the language of those you're engaging with sends a strong message about your commitment.

Includers Make Diversity Central to Their Vision and Mission

Increasingly, corporate America has realized that diversity is a "must-have" value—and today, virtually every company says they "embrace" diversity. It's a nice sentiment, but a true embrace can't just be a core value slapped on the "About Us" section of your website next to teamwork and responsibility. Includers recognize that embracing diversity has to be central to what their organization does and actually part of its vision and mission. Doing so motivates the entire organization, gives employees a higher purpose, and resonates with culturally diverse markets.

But how do you do it? Over the years, I've worked with numerous organizations, helping them do a better job of communicating a diversity, equity, and inclusion vision into their company culture. I've found that one of the most effective ways of doing that is to spend a day or so leading an off-site session with the company. Ideally, it's attended by more than just the leadership, which is, more often than not, white and male. If everyone from the company cannot attend—because they're too busy or the company is too big—I request a range of employees, from executives to front-line workers.

When we get together, I say right up front that the process should start modeling the inclusive behavior we want to see, and that everyone's voice is welcome and encouraged. Then we get to work. We talk about the company, what makes it unique, and more. But the key to making this work is having a really open dialogue about the purpose of the company and how that ties into diversity, equity, and inclusion. Here's what we discuss:

- Customers Served: Does the company serve diverse communities in a unique way? Should it?

- Equitable or Empowering Impact Created: Does the company's hardware or software drive—or have the potential to drive—equity, perhaps by allowing more people to have a voice online?

- Value Derived from Diverse Employees: Does the company's mission or vision statement explain how the value the company offers is derived from diverse voices and experiences?

Includers should drive a dialogue within the company ranks about why diversity is important to the company's mission. And then they articulate that to the public.

Includers Self-Police When Interviewing Diverse Candidates

In 2022, Brian Flores was an NFL coach in search of a team. At one point, he discovered in a text exchange with New England Patriots coach Bill Belichick that his upcoming interview with the New York Giants was a sham—the team had already decided to hire another coach and was sitting down with him simply to "check the box" and comply with the Rooney Rule, which stipulates that all teams must interview at least two women and/or people of color when seeking to fill prominent positions. When he subsequently filed a lawsuit against the league,

Flores claimed that he and other Black coaches had been systemically discriminated against by multiple teams.

Includers understand that the integrity of an organization's diversity recruitment strategy is central to its long-term strength (see sidebar). In addition, they ask themselves a number of questions when they sit down to interview a diverse finalist for a position. Questions like:

1. **Perceptions.** Are my perceptions about this candidate accurate?

2. **Ignorance.** How might my ignorance about this candidate's differences be influencing our interactions together? How might I handle the situation with someone who is more like myself?

3. **Cultural Differences.** Are cultural differences affecting my ability to interact comfortably with this candidate?

4. **Categorization.** Do I tend to put candidates who are different from me in a different category from other candidates (i.e., "the BIPOC candidate")?

5. **Objectification.** Do I tend to objectify people who are different from me? Can I relate to these individuals as equals?

6. **Organizational Support.** Is my organization ready to support a diverse candidate? Have positive steps been taken to ensure diverse candidates and employees can feel valued and welcome?

AVOIDING "CHECK-THE-BOX" EXERCISES AND SHAM INTERVIEWS WITH DIVERSE CANDIDATES

Of course, none of these questions above matter unless the leader trusts that the organization has an inclusive process for recruiting all candidates. Harvard Business School suggests the following best practices to ensure an unbiased recruitment and interviewing process:[25]

1. Craft inclusive job descriptions that welcome in candidates.

2. Educate interviewers on the benefits of diverse teams to counter "just like me" bias.

3. Provide video interview guidelines in advance.

4. Use the same set of questions for all candidates.

5. Select questions that focus on capabilities.

6. Use work samples to assess skills equitably.

The Commitment to Be Inclusive

At the end of the day, we are all on a journey to be Includers. We are faced with something new every day . . . something we don't understand that we have to find a way to reconcile with our accepted belief system. That's human. That's natural.

What makes us accomplices in the fight for anti-racism is not only the depth of our feelings but the strength of our commitments. Some are easy, some are more challenging. But there is so much more each of us can do, as inclusive leaders, to begin that journey. It takes getting started today and committing to finish.

Committing to diversity, equity, and inclusion is an ongoing process with ongoing outcomes. A diverse board of directors sets you apart from businesses that have not done the same and lets employees and your industry know you mean business. Establishing a supplier diversity program shows the small business community you want to embrace them, and committing to culturally specific communications and marketing to those your company serves shows consumers you respect them. Creating a positive DE&I reputation within your industry and among your employees, suppliers, and consumers empowers you and your company and increases your bottom line.

DE&I Best Practices to Keep in Mind

Of all the companies I've worked with over the years, I've found that there are three key elements to transitioning from a general commitment to inclusion to actually implementing a successful diversity, equity, and inclusion program. They are:

- **Empowerment.** Includers empower those around them to share their commitment across the organization. Empowering means:
  - *Involving leadership and cultural influencers in the organization.* Making sure that everyone has a role to play in the inclusion effort can be a powerful way of getting everyone on board.

  - *Building an action plan.* A plan that involves and engages the whole organization with timelines and benchmarks is key to making the effort real.

  - *Communicating the purpose and value of the effort.* Keeping everyone in the loop ensures that the whole organization feels a sense of responsibility and commitment.

- **Taking Action.** Includers also know that commitment requires tangible action with concrete outcomes. Taking action means:
  - *Implementing the action plan.* Move from concept to reality without letting the process drag out. Results matter.

  - *Investing resources in implementation.* That includes financial resources, human resources, and time. Without this trio of resources, DE&I commitments rarely get off the ground.

  - *Communicating progress on implementation.* This doesn't mean overwhelming people with information, but rather keeping people informed and updated on an ongoing, regular basis—not only about the plan's progress but also about how it impacts their business and bottom lines.

- **Accountability.** Includers hold everyone—including themselves—accountable. Creating real accountability means:
  - *Creating success indicators.* This helps employees understand what success looks like. These may be tweaked and refined over

time, but they should be understandable to the organization as a whole, not just those directly responsible. Measurable success indicators show progress and momentum and make diversity, equity, and inclusion real for the whole team.

◦ *Creating a process for learning.* Creating a more inclusive workplace is a journey, and helping employees understand how inclusion impacts the organization, its growth, and financial success is critical. DE&I experts can help here with presentations, updates, and trainings. Again, everyone in the organization, from the boardroom to the mailroom, should be a part of these learnings.

◦ *Communicate success and challenges.* Celebrating success and accomplishments but also immediately addressing challenges can go a long way toward ensuring employees embrace and understand that each person in the company is responsible for diversity, equity, and inclusion—not just HR or the DE&I office.

CHECKLIST: WAYS LEADERS CAN DEMONSTRATE DE&I COMMITMENT AT A GLANCE

Actions speak louder than words. Executives looking for ways to demonstrate their commitment to diversity, equity, and inclusion should consider the following actions:

- **Show C-Suite Commitment.** Appoint a credible Chief Diversity and Inclusion Officer and empower them to implement a comprehensive organization-wide DE&I strategy.

- **Communicate.** Develop an internal and external strategy for communicating about diversity and update key internal and external stakeholders on company DE&I happenings and significant events.

- **Leverage ERGs and DE&I Councils.** Leverage employee resource networks and professional affinity groups; invite employees across all levels of your company to serve on DE&I teams/councils and engage them to serve as Diversity Ambassadors across business lines.

- **Demonstrate Shared Commitment.** Create an initiative or annual DE&I project that engages all employees; participate as the CEO or executive director.

- **Share Knowledge and Thought Leadership.** Create an internal speaker DE&I series featuring thought leaders and experts; participate in select DE&I conferences and webinars—and communicate about what you learn.

- **Forge Partnerships.** Form partnerships with community organizations and NGOs aligned with your DE&I goals.

Includers Think About Their Stakeholders with a DE&I Lens

Includers understand that for diversity to be successful, it has to include all of their stakeholders—and be integrated into the business's overall strategy. Below are some ways leaders can organize their DE&I efforts, ensuring the organization isn't siloed in how its strategy is implemented.

Stakeholders Today

How Includers Embed DE&I Within Their Organization and Stakeholder Relationships

BIPOC, women, and LGBTQ suppliers and vendors

External communications that share the value of DE&I and best practices

Recruitment that attracts, engages, and retains diverse employees

INCLUDER

Internal communications

Charitable gifts and community engagement efforts that address community inequities and create pathways to professional inclusion

Customers and clients who become brand ambassadors and validators for an organization's commitment to DE&I

Networks, diversity councils, and employee resource groups that engage the whole organization in DE&I

How Includers Can Support Their Workforce During an Inequality Uproar

As we have seen all too often, despite all our planning and good intentions as leaders, racial inequality is the "gift that keeps on giving." It seems like every few weeks, another incident becomes national news. Leaders don't have to respond to every racist incident the way they did with George Floyd, but they should be conscious of how these incidents impact their employees.

My friend JocCole "JC" Burton, who has served as a CEO of successful construction businesses in places like Boston and Atlanta, has a terrific playbook for how leaders can support a diverse workforce during a racial inequality uproar. They include:

1. **Provide space for processing.** This can include everything from a roundtable to even a little extra break time for reflection and sharing.

2. **Quickly communicate.** This might be a corporate letter or a short email from the C-suite to employees confirming values and culture.

3.   **Listen.** Allow yourself to hear the heartbreak
     and the fear some employees might have for their
     own personal safety or their children's.

4.   **Check in with HR.** Take a fresh look at diversity
     HR policies, particularly addressing time off and
     mental health breaks.

5.   **Affirm the contributions of diverse team
     members.** Reassuring diverse communities that
     their efforts are valued and needed is critical.

6.   **Commit to ending racial inequities.** Consider
     how you can contribute to positive change, as
     well as how inequity and microaggressions in
     the workplace can negatively impact diverse
     employees.

Super Includers

SEVEN LEADERS WHO BECAME CHAMPIONS FOR ANTI-RACISM

Throughout this book, I've cited a number of white male leaders I know and/or admire for their allyship and leadership on diversity, equity, and inclusion. I've talked about how their practices and examples align with the "seven Cs." While I've cited a number of different leaders, they are hardly the only ones who deserve the moniker of Includer. Whether it is someone like John Landgraf, the Chairman of FX who greenlighted shows like Donald Glover's *Atlanta* with an all-Black writing staff; Jerry Dunfey, a Boston-based hotelier and the son of Irish immigrants who has relentlessly championed Black and female political candidates; or Dale Hansen, former sportscaster at WFAA-TV in Dallas, Texas, who has been a candid critic of the too often regressive policies of

Texas's favorite sport—football—each of these men are Includers in their own right.

But some have taken it even further—either by making anti-racism central to their brand as executives and leaders or, on the other hand, by powerfully demonstrating how to simply "walk the talk" when it comes to diversity. I call them "Super Includers"—white male leaders who for a variety of reasons and in a number of ways have become racial equity and inclusion champions.

Below are seven leaders who all share two things in common. First, they care deeply about inclusion and are committed to taking courageous steps to move the needle at their own personal and professional risk. Second, none of them come from backgrounds that would suggest that they would be particularly committed to racial equity. For me, that is in some ways the most powerful aspect of their stories: that they have taken up the mantle of anti-racism on their own.

I've tried to highlight men many potential allies could identify with: coaches, executives, and policymakers. Some are sons of privilege while others came to prominence pulling themselves up by the bootstraps. In other words, they're people in whom we can see ourselves.

Tim Ryan: The Accountant

At first blush, very little about Tim Ryan's background would make you think he'd one day become a champion for diversity, equity, and inclusion at accounting giant PwC—or bring together 1,600 top executives as part of the CEO Action for Diversity & Inclusion pledge to advance this cause in the workplace.

But if you look closely at Tim's background and formative experiences, you see a man who often felt like an outsider culturally—and used those feelings to make a difference when he rose to the top.

Growing up in Boston during busing before moving to Dedham, a lower-middle-class Boston suburb, Tim's family never had much. His father worked three different jobs. He was a power-line worker at the Boston Edison energy company and moonlighted at the *Boston Herald*, one of the two newspapers in the city. Both jobs had workforces that would frequently go on strike, at which point Tim's dad would pick up some extra cash by working as a garbageman. His mother worked at Roche Bros., a local supermarket chain, where Tim would also get a job at fourteen by lying about his age. Those experiences taught him the value of hard work—and to hustle when he didn't have much.

One formative experience in Tim's life happened at the grocery store when he was a teen. He and his coworker friend were mocking another worker with special needs who was slowly working in the produce section. His manager sternly reprimanded them by saying, "He's giving me his 100%. Are you?" It taught Tim an early lesson about the role of leadership in the workplace, how to create a space where people can be comfortable with their differences, and why inclusive leaders often inspire more productivity from their employees. As Tim would later write, "[If] I don't create an open and empathetic workplace, where people are free to both share their feelings and listen to the perspectives of others, my other priorities—namely, how effectively we serve our clients—will suffer."[26]

He also learned what it felt like to be an outsider as the first member of his family to pursue college. He chose Babson College in nearby Wellesley. In stark contrast to the wealthier kids he went to school with, Tim's dad dropped him off with little more than an old Army duffel bag filled with his possessions. He later said, "I grew up in a working-class community where we were all pretty much the same. Both in the classroom and outside of the classroom, Babson helped me realize that the world is a much bigger, more complex place."[27]

In the workplace, Tim learned early on the impact Includers could have when he took a job at accounting powerhouse PwC right after graduating with a degree in accounting and communications. While being trained with other new hires on a hot day in the office, he realized the short-sleeved shirts he and his mom had picked up at Sears were all wrong—that the other people in the office wore longer sleeves they could roll up when they took their jackets off. Rather than reveal his faux pas, Tim kept his jacket on, sweltering in the summer heat until he could bear it no longer and finally took off his jacket. As he told *Fortune*, "[It was] then I really melted. They were like, 'Who is this kid?'" Thankfully, he was saved by his instructor, who took Tim to buy the right shirts during lunch.

Tim has kept learning about diversity, equity, and inclusion on the job. Virtually the moment he was made CEO of PwC in 2016, the fatal shootings of Alton Sterling, Philando Castile, and police officers in Dallas caused him to immediately pivot his business plan and take the dramatic step of closing PwC for a day to have an all-hands-on-deck discussion on race. Prompted by a Black employee, he started CEO Action as a platform for using PwC's relationship with other CEOs and boards to share best practices on inclusion.

Under Tim's leadership, PwC released detailed diversity data. He said, "I think we're going through a golden age of transparency, and you need to lead by example.

And I like the pressure. We made that decision because we wanted to lead, and we wanted to give others the courage to go. And if you're waiting for the perfect story, it's never going to be there."[28]

Pete Carroll: The Motivator

The NFL has had a long, well-documented history of discrimination. For decades it was a whites-only league, with no Black quarterbacks until 1968 or Black head coaches until Art Shell in 1989. Even today, the NFL has never had a Black owner. We were reminded of this history when the Miami Dolphins' recently fired head coach, Brian Flores, sued the NFL in 2022 for systemic racism that he argued had denied him equal access to head coaching jobs.

For decades, Pete Carroll has been the exception in football leadership ranks: a white man who understands and empathizes with Black players and coaches who are often shut out of the on- and off-field opportunities that are made available to their white colleagues.

The descendant of Irish and Croatian immigrants, Pete knows a thing or two about being underestimated. He also grew up very undersized, which caused him frustration. Even still, he overcame these odds to be a star high school football player.

After college, it became clear to Pete that his playing career was over. But his college coach at Pacific University recognized Pete had an infectious enthusiasm—and offered him an assistant spot on his staff.

Pete worked his way up at a few different programs as an assistant, eventually transitioning to the NFL as an assistant, and then head coach.

In 2001, he went to University of Southern California, setting the stage for one of the greatest college football teams of all time, with players like Reggie Bush and Matt Leinart. The team won two national championships and four Rose Bowls.

It was at USC that Pete began to develop a consciousness around race. Of course, Los Angeles had a notorious history of racial inequity and gang violence, boiling over in the '90s with the beating of Rodney King and the subsequent anti-police riots. LA was also the musical and cultural home of "gangster rap"—which was vilified by the older, white elements of society, despite its incredible popularity with both white and Black young people.

This was the music Pete's players listened to. The music reflected *their* reality and that of urban LA where his star player, and Heisman Trophy winner, Reggie Bush, came from.

Even though Pete was one of those older white guys, he came to recognize the need to celebrate his players' culture and the importance of lifting up their communities and the LA community in particular.

For Pete, it all came to a head one day when he was driving home and heard on the news about another child lost to gang violence. He decided to found A Better LA—a nonprofit dedicated to addressing the determinants of violence in urban Los Angeles, from education and safety, to mental health and homelessness, to poverty and economic infrastructure. Pete recognized that the wealth gap and socioeconomic chasm were barriers to young people he coached, many of whom came from impoverished backgrounds.

When Pete returned to the NFL as head coach of the Seattle Seahawks in 2010, his cultural intelligence helped him connect with players in a way that he hadn't during his first run in the NFL. This ability led to an extended period of success in Seattle.

In 2013, Pete won a Super Bowl with Russell Wilson as quarterback. Wilson is one of only three Black quarterbacks to have ever won a Super Bowl. (Two came in the last decade, reflecting a potentially changing attitude across the league.) Black men were often overlooked for the quarterback position, the focal point of the game. But Pete saw great potential in the also-undersized Wilson—drafting him in the third round. Pete's faith in Wilson, and their subsequent Super Bowl victory, demonstrated what is possible when Black quarterbacks are given the same faith and tools to succeed as white QBs. In fact, under Pete, Wilson was named to nine Pro Bowls.

Pete's cultural IQ also was critical during the racial reckoning following George Floyd's murder. Recognizing the impact it had on players throughout the NFL—a majority of whom are Black—Pete hosted a town hall meeting with his team during the preseason in August 2020, to discuss the emotional toll of the trauma. Instead of trying to "solve the problem" himself and be a white savior, Pete took a back seat and committed to listening and understanding how he can be a better ally, allowing his players to share their raw emotions.

The meeting ended with the players voting not to practice that day, instead deciding that all of them would register to vote before leaving the facility.

At a press conference afterward, Pete expounded on the role he felt he had to play as a white ally. "[White people] need to be coached up and they need to be educated about what the heck is going on in this world," Pete said. "Black people can't scream anymore, they can't march anymore, they can't bare their souls anymore to what they've lived with for hundreds of years."

He went on to say, "White guys came over from Europe and started a new country with a great idea and great ideals and wrote down great writings and laws and all of that, about democracy and freedom and equality for all. And then that's not what happened, because we went down this other road here. We followed economics—and rich white guys making money—and they put together [a] system of slavery, and we've never left it, really. It has never gone away."[29]

His comments spoke to the challenges of the NFL and what needs to change: the fact that there are no Black owners and white people are profiting off of the bodies of Black men who provide a spectacle of entertainment to the detriment of their own health and lives.

Just as important is the message Pete sent by leading from behind—by giving his players agency to express themselves in an open and safe environment, knowing Pete wasn't going to judge them or undermine them professionally or personally. Not only has that trust and credibility Pete has built with his diverse players and coaches impacted them, but it's also the reason he is the oldest coach in the NFL and one of its most successful.

Bob Rivers: The Banker

As a kid, Bob Rivers didn't seem like the prodigal son who would return to his hometown to become one of its foremost C-suite champions of diversity, equity, and inclusion. A devout Catholic, Bob grew up in a very religious, socially conservative family near Boston. He was so shy as a boy that his mother forced him to become an altar boy, figuring that the experience would get him comfortable in front of crowds. Shyness aside, Bob was disciplined and had a strong work ethic. Every morning he woke up early to clean the whole house for his mother while she worked, even washing the kitchen floor.

Bob's father encouraged him to get into finance because it was a safe track to follow, and as a good son who followed his parents' wishes, Bob did. Bob was pragmatic: He lived at home while in college and took public transportation to save money as he commuted back and forth.

Bob was also smart and ambitious and was drawn to people like him. He married a developmental biologist, Nancy, and graduated fifth in his business class. After getting his MBA from the University of Rochester, he promised himself that he'd be a bank president by age forty.

During this time, Bob described himself as an "Alex P. Keaton," the young Republican of the eighties sitcom *Family Ties*. Yet even then, Bob noticed inequity, even if he rarely acted on it. At church on Sundays, he couldn't help but note how there were no women in the clergy and how little power the nuns had. This was reflected in his experience in the workplace, where he noticed how much power male executives had over the female bank tellers.

So why did Bob become an anti-racism convert? It's complicated. But when I spoke to him recently, we discussed the murder of Breonna Taylor, and when he talked about realizing how he didn't understand the level of pain that incident and others like it inflict on communities of color, I was struck by what he said: "I was humbled and ashamed by how little I knew."

Shame. It's a powerful emotion for any of us—but particularly for a man who grew up with a deep respect for his mother and the institution of the Catholic church. And it's a feeling Bob has experienced a few important times in his life. Shame that he didn't act on the inequities he saw with his own eyes. And perhaps, shame he hadn't noticed that the woman he had been married to was gay. Indeed, it was when Bob learned that Nancy had fallen in love with another woman that he began to doubt the belief system he'd been taught his whole life, and he questioned the order of things in his workplace and community, particularly around diversity.

But he also saw something else in diversity: opportunity for his business and unrealized potential in his employees.

At Eastern Bank in Boston, Bob began moving his way up the corporate ladder—becoming its president in

2006 and diving into philanthropy and activism. But it was when Bob championed Eastern's acquisition of Wainwright Bank & Trust—then known as "Boston's Gay Bank" because its CEO, Bob Glassman, had prominently advocated for the gay community in the midst of the HIV epidemic—that he began to distinguish his business by reaching into new communities and tapping into new markets.

Bob also began intentionally expanding his network to break into what he called "the New Boston." As he told me, "I wasn't really willing to play the elite white guy games . . . keeping it the same, not wanting to shake things up. Instead of trying to curry favor with the Old Boston power structure, I was trying to establish relationships with the New Boston—people of color, the LGBTQ community. I knew it would be good for business and for me personally."

Bob also knew he had to have a "ground game" to meet people face to face. When several business leaders came together to form the Black Economic Council of Massachusetts, one thousand people filled Dorchester's Prince Hall auditorium. Bob joined them. Looking every bit the stereotypical white male banker in his suit, Bob was among the only white men there, for the first time feeling very much what it was like to be "the other."

"Honestly, it was thrilling. There weren't a lot of faces I knew," Bob told me. "Most people were asking, 'Who the hell is he and why is he here?'" When it was time to sit down, Bob told himself, "I'm not gonna sit at the front or the back. I'm going to sit right in the middle."

Staying in the middle of things has been Bob's MO ever since. Upon becoming CEO of Eastern Bank, Bob reached out to Get Konnected! with a cold call to me. Over lunch, he told me that he wanted to diversify his corporate board, which at the time was 92 percent white male. In time, Bob reshaped Eastern's board, which is now over 50 percent women, people of color, and LGBTQ folks. He recruited Quincy Miller, a Black man, to take the job of president and be his successor. And Get Konnected! has become an integral part of his own network.

Bob has continued to push the envelope at Eastern as an outspoken advocate of protecting LGBTQ rights. He also helped create the Foundation for Business Equity to help small minority-owned and other businesses that were severely impacted by the pandemic.

Today, Bob has become the go-to business leader in Boston for all things diversity, equity, and inclusion. He's the CEO other business leaders lean on for advice. They're drawn to him because he has a special talent for bringing anti-racism into a business's strategy and its culture.

"It's critical for people to understand why it's important to business," he says of diversity. "Early on, I knew I had to be mindful of it not being my pet project. As CEO, people will follow along, but you have to ingrain it into your culture. It needs to be integrated into business, so that people who disagree with you will still go along."

Justin Trudeau: The Scion

Justin Trudeau knows a thing or two about white male privilege. You might say he embodies the concept. The son of former Canadian Prime Minister Pierre Trudeau, he was born while his dad was in office and surrounded by media attention virtually from birth. But with privilege came responsibility to live up to the ideals of his liberal father and progressive, feminist mother. As a world leader, he has demonstrated how sons of privilege can use their position to advocate for and effect change. And for that reason, he is one of my favorite Super Includers.

Justin's journey to power began at a very young age. Before he had even turned a year old, US President Richard Nixon supposedly said at a gala hosted by his parents, "I'd like to toast the future prime minister of Canada: to Justin Pierre Trudeau"—to which his father replied that he hoped Justin would have Nixon's "grace and skill" to lead. (Thankfully, he did a little better than that!)[30]

His path to being a Super Includer started early as well. Justin's mother wanted to ground him in reality. Though he was initially enrolled in a ritzy private school, she insisted he go to public school, in part because she wanted him to ride the bus every day. The experience provided him with an understanding of life outside the bubble of privilege.

The experience also gave him a passion for education. After graduating from McGill University, he worked as a math and substitute teacher in Vancouver in both private and public schools, working closely with students of different cultures and socioeconomic backgrounds. But he also saw the difference he could make in their lives from his perch through actions as simple as a comment on a test or a side conversation with another teacher.

It was the death of his brother in an avalanche in 1998, and the moving eulogy he gave at his father's funeral in 2000, that thrust Justin into the spotlight, motivating him to get into the family business of politics.

But it was a rally he organized in Toronto in 2006 that showed that Justin would be a different kind of leader than his liberal, yet older-generation father. Led by the former head of a UN peacekeeping force during the Rwandan genocide, the rally urged Canada to respond to the Darfur crisis, demonstrating empathy and sensitivity for those suffering in Sudan. He believed his country needed to step up their game, and in his remarks to the crowd of young people, Justin said, "Canada has coasted a long time on its reputation as peacekeeper. But now we need to follow up with a commitment to protect."

When he was elected to Parliament in 2008, Justin was acutely aware that expectations were high. He said, "Dealing with being my father's son isn't something that I suddenly had to get my mind around as I showed up in this place as an MP . . . it's been something that's been with me all my life."

But he knew if he picked up his father's mantle, he would have to forge his own path and raise the bar.

Virtually from the moment he was named leader of Canada's liberal party in 2013, Justin met the moment, embracing diversity, gender equity, and immigration—using his position to set an example. In 2015, he tweeted, "I am a feminist. I'm proud to be a feminist. #upfordebate"—and tied it back to his upbringing.

He said, "My mom raised me to be a feminist. My father raised me, he was a different generation, but he raised me to respect and defend everyone's rights, and I deeply grounded my own identity in that, and I am proud to say that I am a feminist."[31]

Justin's embrace of feminism wasn't virtue signaling. The young leader clearly thought making the Liberal Party the feminist party in Canada was good for business, as it were. "I am perfectly comfortable with Canadians knowing that the Liberal Party is unequivocal in its defense of women's rights," he said. "We are the party of the Charter. We are the party that stands up for people's rights. We will continue to do so."[32]

As prime minister, he put his money where his mouth was on diversity, investing $400 million to provide loans up to $250,000 to Black business owners and entrepreneurs across the country and spending taxpayer dollars to collect more detailed data and research on women, Indigenous people, and racialized communities. He also pledged to admit one million refugees over three years.

Justin did all this because he thought it was the right thing to do, but also because he had advisors that looked like Canada, where one in five people—and half of Toronto—were foreign-born. So he surrounded himself with the most ethnically diverse and gender-diverse cabinet in the country's history.

However, with diversity has come debate and dissent. Trudeau's administration has had no shortage of allies speak up in disagreement with him on a range of issues. One minister openly criticized the NAFTA trade agreement, while members of his party have frequently spoken up about the need for their leader to push harder on other diversity issues.

Indeed, Justin embodies a key quality of Super Includers: not only taking action but also embracing "soft skills" such as being unafraid to show deference to others and even to share power. Indeed, not long after becoming party leader, he gave up his seat at Nelson Mandela's funeral for a fellow party representative who had long worked with Mandela to end apartheid. Though a small gesture, it was a powerful example of Justin's humility and ability to subjugate his own ego in recognition of others and their commitment to equality.

Of course, some may question my selection of Justin Trudeau as a Super Includer because of the brownface controversy in 2019, which I mentioned earlier in this book. But it was how he responded to this scandal that demonstrated Justin's Super Includer bona fides. Owning his mistake fully, he said, "I shouldn't have done that. I should have known better, but I didn't. And I'm really sorry."

When asked if he thought the photograph was racist, he didn't equivocate: "Yes, it was. I didn't consider it a racist action at the time, but now we know better and this was something that was unacceptable."[33]

Justin also showed that Super Includers put their commitment to inclusion before their self-image. On a trip to India in 2018, when Justin and his family dressed in traditional Indian clothes, their outfits were criticized as "too Indian, even for an Indian." Perhaps it was, but Includers know that being culturally sensitive can sometimes open them up to ridicule or being made fun of—and that's okay.

As the son of power and privilege, Justin Trudeau understands something critical: that the white men who have most of the control of our economy, government, and society are of an older generation and time and that needs have changed. As he later said, "We need to recognize that for Indigenous peoples, the Canadian reality has not been—and is not today—easy, equitable, or fair. We need to acknowledge that our history includes darker moments: the Chinese head tax; the internment of Ukrainian, Japanese, and Italian Canadians during the First and Second World Wars; our turning away boats of Jewish or Punjabi refugees; our own history of slavery."[34]

That's Justin Trudeau. Rather than defend the past out of guilt or to hold on to power, he knows it is better to *learn* from past mistakes, own up to them, and set a more inclusive path. That as we condemn the past we can also teach and change the future.

"I think we can aim a little higher than mere tolerance," Trudeau said about interactions with those different from us. "Think about it: Saying 'I tolerate you' actually means something like, 'Okay, I grudgingly admit that you have a right to exist, just don't get in my face about it, and oh, don't date my sister.' There's not a religion in the world that asks you to 'tolerate thy neighbor.' So let's try for something a little more like acceptance, respect, friendship, and yes, even love. And why does this matter? Because, in our aspiration to relevance; in our love for our families; in our desire to contribute, to make this world a better place, despite our differences, we are all the same.

"We are not going to arrive at mutual respect, which is where we solve common problems, if we cocoon ourselves in an ideological, social, or intellectual bubble."[35]

Ultimately, what makes Justin Trudeau a Super Includer most is that he has walked the walk on diversity. He understands the obligation leaders have to move us forward on these difficult issues—even when it isn't convenient. Never was this clearer than after George Floyd's murder, when Justin took a knee at Black Lives Matter protests in Ottawa. Justin's gesture was a powerful symbol, and it was all the more remarkable because it came on the heels of criticism that he had avoided commenting on Donald Trump's violent reaction to the BLM protests.

While his twenty-one-second pause at a press conference where he was asked to denounce Trump's tear-gassing of protesters got most of the press's attention, what struck me most was Justin's full-throated embrace of allyship that followed:

> *We all watch in horror and consternation what's going on in the United States. It is a time to pull people together, but it is a time to listen, it is time to learn what injustices continue despite progress over years and decades. But it is a time for us as Canadians to recognize that we too have our challenges. That Black Canadians and racialized Canadians face discrimination as a lived reality every single day. There is systemic discrimination in Canada, which means our systems treat Canadians of color, Canadians who are racialized, differently than they do others. It is something that many of us don't see, but it is something that is a lived reality for racialized Canadians. We need to see that, not just as a government, and take action, but we need to see that as Canadians.*
>
> *We need to be allies in the fight against discrimination. We need to listen. We need to learn, and we need to work hard to figure out how we can be part of the solution on fixing things. This government has done a number of things over the past years, but there's lots more to do, and we will continue to do that because we see, we see you, we see the discrimination that racialized Canadians live every single day.[36]*

Showing humility. Imploring people to listen. Acknowledging uncomfortable truths. Articulating what can and must be done to propel us forward. That is what Justin Trudeau has shown. And it is what Super Includers do.

Richard Branson: The Entrepreneur

Richard Branson is certainly one of the most well-known billionaires in the world. The head of Virgin Group, the loquacious Brit is eminently recognizable for his long-flowing blond hair, chatty media personality, and zany stunts involving hot air balloons, and, more recently, space flight. But he has also spent much of his life fighting for equality, demonstrating why inclusion and anti-racism can be an integral part of a successful businessman's brand.

In many ways, Richard was destined to be a success. Born into an upper-middle-class family in a nice area of South London, his father was an attorney and his mother was a ballet dancer and entrepreneur with a myriad of side hustles—building and selling everything from wooden tissue boxes to wastepaper bins.

But in other ways, young Richard had the cards stacked against him. He struggled with ADHD and dyslexia so much so that a teacher once told him he'd either end up a millionaire or in prison due to his obvious potential but poor academic performance. In the '50s and '60s, there was virtually no support or proper teaching techniques for someone with dyslexia. For Richard, it was an early lesson in seeing how not everyone is born with equal opportunities.

Why is Richard Branson a Super Includer? For someone who grew up in a successful family, Richard has exercised an especially remarkable innate sense of fairness and level of acknowledgment that you should treat people with respect. Having myself grown up in a British culture, I've seen the class snobbery that leads families to distance themselves from members who they think have "married down." As the old saying goes, money doesn't buy you class. But in Richard Branson's case, his dyslexia perhaps gave him a window to what it's like to be "other."

From his mother, Richard inherited that entrepreneurial spirit of risk-taking. Hustling from the jump as a young man, he was drawn to the rock music scene as it was exploding in late '60s London—starting a magazine in a church basement, selling records by mail order before opening a brick-and-mortar store, and eventually opening a recording studio, which became Virgin Records in 1972.

After a customs and tax scheme almost landed him in prison, Richard wanted to try something new. He built the Virgin Records empire by breaking the mold, releasing *Tubular Bells* by Mike Oldfield—a forty-minute instrumental piece performed entirely by one artist . . . that sold millions of copies. Riding the tide of progressive rock and roll music in the UK, Virgin often featured music that was experimental and embraced cultural issues like homophobia, sexism, racism, and the anti-war movement—famously releasing the Sex Pistols' punk rock record, *Never Mind the Bollocks, Here's the Sex Pistols.*

Richard was an early pioneer in understanding that inclusion could sell. Where many more "established" record labels were turned off by artists pushing barriers, he openly embraced progressivism and marginalized communities. By the 1980s, one of Virgin's most commercially successful artists was Culture Club, fronted by cross-dressing Boy George. Richard took him in at a time when the singer was at a low point, struggling with addiction and a breakup from his boyfriend, which was not yet public news. Virgin would go on to release records by a diverse array of artists including Paula Abdul, Lenny Kravitz, and Janet Jackson, the latter of whom he offered the largest record contract in history.

But Richard's tendency to "go against the grain" and embrace diversity was not only for the artists he signed.

It's also how he ran his business. In an interview with *Mint*, Richard said, "Diversity is an advantage for any company and can be an important factor in its success . . . Employing people from different backgrounds and who have various skills, viewpoints and personalities will help you to spot opportunities, anticipate problems and come up with original solutions before your competitors do." By contrast, he said, "An entrepreneur who hires a lot of people who are just like her and have had the same experiences will find that she's leading a team that is less creative and helpful to customers, and ultimately produces lower profits."

Richard has also long been a champion of the LGBTQ community specifically. In 1982, he bought London's world-renowned gay nightclub Heaven, which remained in the Virgin "family" for over twenty-five years. At the Virgin Group, Richard recognized the pressure his LGBTQ employees were under. As he told *Mint*, "[LGBTQ] people working in unfriendly environments reported feeling depressed (34%), distracted (27%) and exhausted (23%), while those who reported feeling isolated at work were 73% more likely to say they were planning to leave their companies within three years. A company's best assets are its people, and if a significant portion of them are getting ready to leave, that's an emergency that needs your attention."[37]

Inclusion has been a part of Richard's personal core values from the get-go, as evidenced by his company's strong commitment to diversity, equity, and inclusion, even pre-#MeToo and pre–George Floyd's death.

One of Richard's most visible commitments to inclusion was his relationship with Nelson Mandela, who influenced his life significantly. In 2007, along with musician Peter Gabriel, the two founded The Elders—a nonprofit advocating for humanitarian issues, which Richard continues to support through funding and through his seat on its Advisory Council. In 2020, he announced a commitment from Virgin to The Bail Project, and he has long been an advocate for ending the death penalty and decriminalizing drugs, both of which are issues that disproportionately affect the Black community.

Richard continues to rebel in ways big and small, flying into space in 2022 with a space travel company. But even as he was criticized for Virgin Galactic, he has continued to deepen his commitment to equality and inclusion here on Earth.

Recently, Richard has also opened up about how his own experience with dyslexia has pushed him to think about the needs of building a "neurodiverse workforce" to help solve big problems. As a result, Richard invested in an IT company called auticon that pushes global businesses to employ autistic people as technology consultants. Richard made two Virgin businesses clients of theirs, and pushed the company to train their employees, managers, and recruiters on developing workplaces inclusive of neurodiversity.

Sharing personal stories of autistic technologists on his blog, Richard wrote: "I think their experiences really show how hiring a neurodiverse team can benefit your business—and the lives of people who may think a little differently to you. It's also a reminder to all of us to search for the things that unite us in our common humanity, rather than the things that divide us."[38]

Richard Branson: always hustling, always pushing in new directions and always—*always*—getting attention. When it comes to inclusion, we need more allies like him.

Ray Mabus: The Southerner

I have a dream that one day even the state of Mississippi, a desert state, sweltering with the heat of injustice and oppression, will be transformed into an oasis of freedom and justice.

—Martin Luther King Jr., August 28, 1963

Of all the states in the union, perhaps none is known for being more hostile toward people of color than Mississippi. In many ways the epicenter of Jim Crow, the state—where four in ten citizens are Black—is viewed as synonymous with vehement segregationists and horrific imagery of bombs, dogs, and fires set against children.

This was the environment fourth-generation Southerner Ray Mabus was born into in 1948. Ray's father came from a dirt-poor family. Despite growing up without electricity and running water, his father went on to earn a degree in engineering, open his own hardware store, and eventually return to school to receive a degree in philosophy.

Ray shared his father's commitment to educational excellence, graduating summa cum laude from the University of Mississippi, before going on to receive his master's degree in political science from Johns Hopkins and his law degree from Harvard Law. Those experiences—in the Deep South but also urban Baltimore and starchy New England—gave Ray a broad perspective on society as well as on inclusion, integration, and diversity.

But from a young age, education and civil rights were inextricably linked in Ray's life. Recalling the 1962 Ole Miss riot that attempted to prevent the enrollment of James Meredith as the university's first Black student when Ray was in ninth grade, he said, "That Monday morning after the riot—it was the talk of my school, and I came home that afternoon and said something I had heard at school—something smart—to my father and he sat me down and talked to me for two hours about the rule of law, about the inherent equality of people, about how not to judge people on things like skin color but to judge them on ability and individuality."[39]

At the University of Mississippi, Ray was further exposed to the harsh realities of racism, with the school's athletic teams competing as the Ole Miss Rebels (which they continue to do today). On the evening of Dr. King's assassination in 1968, when Ray was a junior, the president of his fraternity used a racial slur, which caused Ray to walk out and never speak to the upperclassman again. As he says today, "In '68, we had the same level of frustration, anger, and racism in our society as today. But we have more universal outpouring now—back then, no one was talking about ending systemic racism."

By then, Ray had already caught the political bug. In 1967, Ray volunteered on William Winter's first gubernatorial campaign. While Winter wasn't as vocal an opponent of segregation as Ray, the two shared a belief that education was the key to unlocking opportunity and creating a more level playing field for all people.

Winter's 1967 campaign for governor was unsuccessful, but Ray was Winter's legal counsel when he won in 1979. While in office, Winter sought to overhaul the public education system, which was no easy task in post-desegregation Mississippi. Ray was one of several

young aides—mockingly dubbed the "Boys of Spring"—
who lectured across the state to build popular support
for the education initiative, which ultimately proved
successful.

When Ray was elected governor of Mississippi in
1988, at the age of thirty-nine, he was the youngest governor in the country. He made education a priority, giving teachers the largest pay raise of any profession in the
state, which contrasted starkly with most policies in the
Deep South.

"We have to value education more highly," he would
later say. "The only way up, the only way to improve is
through better education, and not just better education
for a few, but better education for everyone—and if we
don't do that, we're going to be consigned to be at or near
the bottom forever."[40]

One issue Ray didn't tackle as governor—which he
would later regret—was changing the state flag, which
included the Confederate battle flag until 2021. He later
noted that while he was governor, he wasn't aware "of
how hurtful it was, what a bad symbol it was, how evil
the things it represented were."[41] Ray's advocacy later in
life not only showed a change of heart—but a willingness
to learn from his mistakes, a key quality in Includers.

In 2009, Ray was nominated to be President Obama's
first Secretary of the Navy, in which he had served before

attending law school in the 1970s. One of the more cere-
monial responsibilities of the Navy Secretary is to name
ships in the naval fleet. In many ways, he had every reason to go along and get along. Instead, Ray surprised a
lot of people by naming naval ships after civil and gay
rights icons.

The criticism was swift and fierce, with some, like
Retired Vice Admiral Doug Crowder, describing Ray as
making a political statement: "It just doesn't help at all
for what the basic sailor or officer thinks of his chain of
command, up to the Secretary of the Navy."

Ray was unapologetic, saying, "I have named ships
after presidents. I have named ships after members of
Congress who have been forceful advocates for the Navy
and Marine Corps. But I think you have to represent all
the values that we hold as Americans, that we hold as a
country. And so that's why I've named ships the *Med-
gar Evers*, *Cesar Chavez*, *John Lewis*, the *Harvey Milk*.
Because these are American heroes too, just in a different arena."[42]

Ray was just as outspoken about inclusion for LGBTQ
members of the armed forces, calling the policy ban-
ning LGBTQ people in the military "insidious and mor-
ally wrong." As Navy Secretary, he argued the ban used
"flawed logic" that claimed the inclusion of LGBTQ troops
would erode the war-fighting capability of the United

States. "And yet," he said, "the Navy, the Marines, the Army, the Air Force [and the] Coast Guard are the most powerful forces in the world today." Ray said it not only proved "a more diverse force is a stronger force" but that it needed to represent and reflect the nation it defends. Noting that there were 65,000 active-duty LGBTQ members and over a million LGBTQ veterans, Ray also encouraged those discharged under "Don't Ask, Don't Tell" to have their military records reviewed to change the discharge characterization.[43]

Ray also proved that inclusion is good for business and for morale. In 2013, despite all the attention he received over ship naming and LGBTQ policy, Glassdoor ranked Ray among the fifty highest-rated CEOs as part of its Employees' Choice rankings of companies and leaders, ahead of luminaries such as Oracle's Larry Ellison, Dell's Michael Dell, and GE's Jeff Immelt, with an 82 percent approval rating from employees.[44] And of course, Ray's employees weren't progressives from Silicon Valley or Austin—but the men and women of the conservative US military.

After leaving public service, Ray remained laser-focused on championing equality as CEO of consultancy The Mabus Group, helping companies and leaders embrace rather than resist change. In the wake of the 2017 Charlottesville white supremacist rally, Ray pushed for changing Mississippi's state flag and removing Confederate statues. "Events like Charlottesville underscore the truth of William Faulkner's view that in too many places and for too many people 'the past isn't dead; it isn't even past,'" he wrote in *Time*.[45]

Like fellow Southerner Mitch Landrieu (see chapter one), Ray spoke powerfully about the actual post-slavery history of reviving Confederate symbolism to revive oppression: "Removing these memorials and symbols . . . is not an effort to sanitize our history nor erase some part of our culture," he said, going on to cite "the myths of 'magnolias and moonlight,' of 'the benevolent slave owner,' [and] the romantic narratives of 'The Lost Cause'" as "the real efforts to sanitize and erase" the Confederate fight to preserve the right to own slaves.[46]

In many ways, Ray Mabus is a Super Includer because he had every reason not to be one. He was a white male born into the segregated South. Little was handed to him on the road to success, yet, he realized that his privilege and power could be a catalyst for change that benefits and reflects the contributions of everyone. Even today, as he approaches his mid-seventies, Ray continues to blaze that trail.

Seth DeValve: The Jock

Professional sports is one area in society that is both diverse and also a product of systemic racism. Today, most pro sports are very diverse among their players but still have a ways to go when it comes to inclusion of racial and gender diversity, particularly in team ownership and the front office, and on leadership teams. So it often falls to the players to push both owners and the leagues to address issues of diversity, equity, and inclusion. It is in this context that the leadership of Seth DeValve—a former tight end for the Cleveland Browns—has been so important.

Seth grew up in a typical white middle-class home in Manchester, Connecticut. The son of a former long-distance runner, he was a star athlete growing up and a National Guard scholar/athlete in high school.

He attended and played football at Princeton University, a school not known for its football prowess. Seth also battled multiple injuries in both feet, one of which required surgery, throughout his time at Princeton and missed a significant number of games over his five years there. Nonetheless, he was drafted in the fourth round by the Browns in 2016, becoming the highest-selected Princeton player of all time.

While at Princeton, Seth met his wife, Erica Harris, a Black woman, while they were both students. She first noticed him in class, but the two didn't begin to speak until he led a service at the on-campus church to which they both belonged. Their friendship grew through a college ministry group. Seth proposed shortly after his first NFL game, and the couple has been together ever since.

Seth had only been in the NFL for a few months when San Francisco 49ers quarterback Colin Kaepernick quietly began staying seated during the national anthem at the beginning of games. Once the cameras spotlighted Kaepernick's gesture, it sparked controversy among the NFL's largely white and conservative fan base, many of whom saw it as an act of disrespect for the flag and the country.

Kaepernick, on the other hand, saw his gesture as a way of shining a spotlight on racial inequity, in particular how Black people were being killed by law enforcement at a disproportionately high rate. As a Black man, he made a conscious decision to use his celebrity and platform as an NFL player to bring attention to racial injustice. However, at the recommendation of white Army veteran and former long snapper Nate Boyer, he began to kneel instead of sit, as a sign of respect.

Soon after, Black players across the league began kneeling in solidarity with Kaepernick. It was striking that no white players joined their Black teammates in kneeling, and it wasn't hard to understand why. The NFL Commissioner, Roger Goodell, came out against Kaepernick, saying, "I don't necessarily agree with what he is doing . . . I support our players when they want to see change in society, and we don't live in a perfect society. On the other hand, we believe very strongly in patriotism in the NFL. I personally believe very strongly in that."[47]

Goodell's remarks only hinted at the conversations going on behind the scenes, where NFL owners were livid that their players were upsetting their fan base. As a result, during the 2016 season, while players stood in "solidarity" with their Black teammates, no white player took a knee.

A year later, the controversy was reignited after white nationalists marched on Charlottesville, Virginia, and a woman was run over and killed by a car driven into a crowd of anti-racist protesters by a white nationalist. Calls grew for white players to act.

"You need a white guy to join the fight," said Seattle Seahawks defensive end Michael Bennett, coached by Super Includer Pete Carroll. "The white guy is super important to the fight. For people to really see social injustices, there must be someone from the other side of the race who recognizes the problem, because a lot of times if just one race says there's a problem, nobody is realistic about it."[48]

While Seahawks center Justin Britt put his hand on Bennett's shoulder while Bennett sat on the bench and the Eagles' Chris Long put his arm around safety Malcolm Jenkins as Jenkins raised his fist, still no white players kneeled.

Enter Seth DeValve, the second-year tight end married to a Black woman. Though he was not known as an activist, he was inspired by his wife to act, and on August 21, 2017, he joined several Black Browns players in taking a knee during the national anthem—the first white player to kneel.

"I love this country. I love our national anthem," said DeValve. "I'm very grateful to the men and women who have given their lives and give a lot every day to protect this country and to serve this country, and I want to honor them as much as I can. The United States is the greatest country in the world. And it is because it provides opportunities to its citizens that no other country does. The issue is that it doesn't provide equal opportunity to everybody, and I wanted to support my African American teammates today who wanted to take a knee. We wanted to draw attention to the fact that there [are] things in this country that still need to change."[49]

DeValve acknowledged that he had a different perspective than some of his white teammates. "I, myself, will be raising children that don't look like me, and I want to do my part as well to do everything I can to raise them in a better environment than we have right now," he said. "I wanted to take the opportunity with my teammates during the anthem to pray for our country and also to draw attention to the fact that we have work to do. And that's why I did what I did."[50]

Not long after, his wife spoke out in support of her husband—but also made it clear that Seth was not a "white savior," and shouldn't be viewed as such. She said, "To center the focus of Monday's demonstration solely on Seth is to distract from what our real focus should be: listening to the experiences and the voices of the Black people who are using their platforms to continue to bring the issue of racism in the US to the forefront."[51]

She pointed out that Seth, as a white man, never could truly feel the weight and burden of racial discrimination and oppression. But, she added, "All white people should care and take a stand against its prevalence in this country. What I hope to see from this is a shift in the conversation to Seth's Black teammates, who realistically have to carry that burden all the time."

It's important to realize that dismantling systemic racism requires the people who hold the power to make it happen: white men. In that sense, Erica DeValve made a powerful point about what Includers can—and can't—accomplish.

Includers—white allies in leadership—are not "white knights" coming in on their white horses to save people of color. Rather, they are accomplices and advocates who, in solidarity, are willing to "lead from behind" by listening and learning what they can do to create sustainable systemic change.

Notwithstanding Seth's courage and empathy, his gesture only further highlighted the inequity facing Black and white players in the NFL and, more broadly, the American workplace in general. While both Kaepernick and DeValve took a knee during the national anthem to protest racial inequity, Seth went on to have a career playing for four NFL teams, while Kaepernick did not. Indeed, even after Roger Goodell admitted that he wished he had "listened earlier" to Kaepernick in the wake of George Floyd's tragic murder, the Super Bowl veteran quarterback has never played another down in the NFL.

Rather than stoking cynicism, however, the DeValve-Kaepernick disparity should inspire us to action. It clearly underscores the difference white allies can make. And not only that—their actions also demonstrate why we need more Includers to step up and address issues of inequity and racial injustice.

COULD YOU BE A SUPER INCLUDER? TAKE THE SUPER INCLUDER IQ TEST AND FIND OUT

Is being an Includer innate or can it be learned? Well, in most cases it's both—applying the core values we grew up with and the experiences in our lives to fight for others. But as this test shows, some of us are more inclined to be Includers than others. Answer these seven questions and find out how close you are to becoming one.

1. Have I ever felt like an outsider?

2. Would I be willing to share my stories of including and excluding others to help those around me learn?

3. Have I exhibited acts of courage to stand up for and speak out for others at my own personal or professional risk?

4. Have I reflected on difficult questions like "Who would I be without racism?" and "Do my personal behavior and politics perpetuate racism?"

5. Do I view my privilege as an opportunity to build a more just and inclusive world rather than simply a source of guilt and shame?

6. Am I open and willing to learn others' stories of race, racism, and discrimination—and to recognize that they are not my stories?

7. Have I made a personal commitment to taking steps to
    ensure that diversity, equity, and inclusion become a core
    value in my personal and professional life?

Scores: 0–2: "I Have Work to Do." 3–5: "I'm Definitely Includer
Material." 6–7: "I Have Super Includer Potential."

Epilogue

A CLARION CALL TO CORPORATE AMERICA

One name largely missing from this book is possibly the most conspicuous: Donald J. Trump. Of course, his omission was no coincidence, and his inclusion would have subsumed this book, just as he has our country. But as I was finishing this book, I realized that avoiding any discussion of him was no longer possible, especially after the insurrection at the US Capitol on January 6, 2021, and his second impeachment in just over a year.

The sight of white men and women storming our nation's Capitol Building brought many emotions to the fore for all of America, including for me. Some of the images were horrifying—a police officer being crushed by the mob. Others were bizarre—the photographing of the rotunda from within the confines of the velvet ropes, as if on a public tour. And one was reassuring—the image of Officer Eugene Goodman, a Black member of the Capitol Police, cagily leading rioters away from the Senate Chambers before members had evacuated, for which he was subsequently awarded the Congressional Gold Medal.

But the most powerful images, which confirmed for me why this book is so necessary, were those of the police simply allowing insurrectionists to walk into the Capitol, juxtaposed with the violent images of law enforcement and military treatment of peaceful protesters following George Floyd's death the previous summer. As then–President-elect Biden said following the insurrection, "No one can tell me that if it had been a group of Black Lives Matter protest[ers] yesterday they wouldn't have been treated very, very differently than the mob of thugs that stormed the Capitol. We all know that's true. And it is unacceptable. Totally unacceptable. The American people saw it in plain view."[52]

And so did corporate America. With numerous companies—Hallmark, Mastercard, American Express, and Blue Cross Blue Shield among them—announcing they would withhold donations to politicians who had supported the insurrection and sought to disenfranchise millions of voters, most of them Black. While their actions were welcomed and should continue, leaders need not wait until democracy itself is under siege to show leadership on issues of diversity.

As we look ahead, one of the most important lessons to remember is that we cannot depend on politicians to move the dial on diversity, equity, and inclusion in America. It is going to be up to leaders of all stripes to be the allies, accomplices, and advocates for the anti-racism movement and for the dismantling of systemic and structural racism. American business is in a unique position to take action. The vision, talent, and resources of US chief executive offices are unparalleled. Bringing to bear their collective problem-solving skills can go a long way toward creating a proactive equitable business climate that can both improve race relations and offer real solutions to the wealth disparity between white Americans and BIPOC communities.

By bringing people of all racial and ethnic groups more completely into the economic mainstream, corporate America will not only be moving us toward a more economically inclusive and equitable society but will be making a sound investment in its own future. With hope and grace, I believe it can be done.

Additional Resources to Support Diversity, Equity, and Inclusion

Throughout this book, I've shared what I believe to be the best thinking and expertise on how to advance diversity, equity, and inclusion in the workplace. DE&I is a collaborative effort—and if there's anything I've learned it's that there is no one solution to the challenge.

Books for Further Reading

- Robin DiAngelo – *White Fragility: Why It's So Hard for White People to Talk About Racism*

- Ibram X. Kendi – *How to Be an Antiracist*

- Isabel Wilkerson – *Caste*

- Debby Irving – *Waking Up White: And Finding Myself in the Story of Race*

Tools to Advance DE&I

- Included – An employee engagement and people analytics platform to capture and measure diversity, equity, and inclusion performance within organizations

- Get Konnected! – My own cross-cultural business networking event series to curate connections and foster positive business and social relationships

Acknowledgments

It truly takes a village to write a book; and I am forever grateful to those in my village who have inspired, encouraged, and assisted me in writing this book. First is my sister, Roma Phillips Spencer; her husband, Gerry; and their four children, Al Spencer, Romona Spencer-Anderson, Mariella Spencer, and Marcia Spencer-Isaac, who have all served as cheerleaders and avid fans.

Matthew Weiner, I am filled with profound gratitude and deep appreciation for the hours you spent reviewing and editing my many drafts and listening to and helping me recall some of my experiences and lessons learned advising clients. You asked all the right questions and sent me back to my desktop more times than I care to remember to dig a little deeper. It was your assistance that truly helped me capture my own personal business stories, as well as those of the people featured in this book, and convert them into teachable moments and touchpoints.

Andre Porter, my good friend and compadre, I am deeply thankful to you for helping make the right connections to complete this book.

Jelani Bandele, you took this project to the next level. I hold an abundance of appreciation for how you sprang into action bringing an editor's lens and a strong commitment for excellence and accuracy to this project. Your insights, ideas, and probing questions helped me fully capture the essence and important takeaways of each chapter and brought greater clarity to the final manuscript.

Lorin Rees, my agent, to you I extend a huge thanks for introducing me to Glenn Yeffeth, publisher and founder of BenBella Books. Your mother, the late Helen Rees, a mentor and friend who had been encouraging me for years to write a book, would be proud of our collaboration.

To my CPC colleagues Maria DeSimone and Ryan Litner, who assisted in doing research on the Super Includers, I am grateful for and indebted to you for the hard work you do every day to support me and the important work we do on behalf of our clients.

To the Focs (aka Colette's ride or die posse): my attorney, Agnes Bundy Scanlan; my executive coach, Dr. Priscilla Douglas; my mentor, former Massachusetts Lieutenant Governor Evelyn Murphy; Janet

Langhart Cohen, Nancy Korman, and Carol Gold-berg; my dear friends Charlotte Golar Richie, Dr. Sue Windham-Bannister, Dr. Marilyn Griffin, Charlayne Murrell-Smith, and Joyce Gallagher; Mary Helen Gillespie; my Caribbean sisters and brothers includ-ing Karen Hinds (St. Vincent), Jackie Glenn (Jamaica), Juliette Mayers and Barbara Alleyne (Barbados), Judy Niles (Trinidad and Tobago), Dr. Clyde Niles (St. Lucia), and Herby Duverné (Haiti); *New York Times* bestselling author and BU professor Phyllis Karas; and Dr. Yale Pearlson, I am eternally grateful for your enthusiastic inspiration, encouragement, and motivation.

Last, but definitely not least, I offer a sincere thank-you to my publishers Glenn Yeffeth and Adrienne Lang, and the BenBella Books team that brought me across the finish line, including art director Sarah Avinger, produc-tion director Monica Lowry, marketing director Lind-say Marshall, and my two amazing senior editors, Leah Wilson and Vy Tran—the latter of whom sent me back to the drawing board not once but multiple times . . . and guess what? She was spot-on. Though at first, I thought her suggestions would change the essence of the book, her suggestions made for an infinitely more well-written, compelling, and informative book. I also want to thank Joe Rhatigan for his diligent and thoughtful edits and comments throughout.

Notes

1   Katherine Wu, "Study of 17 Million Identifies Crucial Risk Factors for Coronavirus Deaths," *New York Times*, July 8, 2020, https://www.nytimes.com/2020/07/08/health/coronavirus-risk-factors.html.

2   "'Put Simply, It Is Bullying': Prince Harry's Full Statement on the Media," *Guardian*, March 8, 2021, https://www.theguardian.com/uk-news/2019/oct/02/put-simply-its-bullying-prince-harrys-full-statement-on-the-media.

3   Liz Halloran, "Michelle Obama: 'Being President . . . Reveals Who You Are,'" NPR, September 5, 2012, https://www.npr.org/sections/itsallpolitics/2012/09/04/160581747/michelle-obama-being-president-reveals-who-you-are.

4   "Nobel Prizes 2022," NobelPrize.org, n.d., https://www.nobelprize.org/prizes/peace/1986/wiesel/acceptance-speech/.

5   "Mitch Landrieu's Book: 'A White Southerner Confronts History,'" Axios, March 20, 2018, https://www.axios.com/2018/03/20/mitch-landrieu-confederate-statues-racism-america.

6   Stuart Levine et al., "Ursula Burns," *Forbes*, n.d., https://www.forbes.com/profile/ursula-burns/?sh=3c5551e540a0.

7   "Quotations—Martin Luther King, Jr. Memorial (U.S. National Park Service)," n.d., https://www.nps.gov/mlkm/learn/quotations.htm.

8   Zlati Meyer, "With 'Moral Courage,' Starbucks Workers Take Part in Emotional Training to Avoid Racial Bias," *USA Today*, May 30, 2018, https://eu.usatoday.com/story/money/

business/2018/05/29/starbucks-howard-schultz-racial-bias-training-discrimination-african-american/652395002/.

9   Stephen Tisdalle, "State Street Global Advisors CMO on 'Fearless Girl' Lessons," *Wall Street Journal,* November 4, 2018, https://deloitte.wsj.com/articles/state-street-global-advisorscmo-on-fearless-girl-lessons-1541379735.

10 PwC, "Building on a Culture of Belonging, 2020 PwC Diversity & Inclusion Transparency Report," https://www.rdcc.ro/wp-content/uploads/2021/11/https___www.pwc_.com_us_en_about-us_diversity_assets_diversity-inclusion-transparency-report.pdf.

11 Brian Tracy, "The Importance of Honesty and Integrity in Business," *Entrepreneur*, November 2, 2016, https://www.entrepreneur.com/leadership/the-importance-of-honesty-and-integrity-in-business/282957.

12 "How Diversity Can Drive Innovation," *Harvard Business Review*, August 1, 2014, https://hbr.org/2013/12/how-diversity-can-drive-innovation.

13 "AT&T Sorry for Magazine Drawing That Depicted African as Monkey," AP News, September 17, 1993, https://apnews.com/article/60be9c478fbfe5f07a72dae04e3d533f.

14 Joshua Fields, "AT&T CEO Randall Stephenson Addresses the Racial Tension in American Society," YouTube, September 25, 2016, https://www.youtube.com/watch?v=ThO74-oFt_Q.

15 Ibid.

16 "Emotional and Cultural Intelligence in Leaders," Western Governors University Blog, October 22, 2018, https://www.wgu.edu/blog/emotional-cultural-intelligence-leaders1810.html.

17 Blue Cross Blue Shield Massachusetts, "Health Equity Report," https://www.bluecrossma.org/myblue/equity-in-health-care/health-equity-report.

18 Loretta J. Ross, "What if Instead of Calling People Out, We Called Them In?" *New York Times*, November 19, 2020, https://www.nytimes.com/2020/11/19/style/loretta-ross-smith-college-cancel-culture.html.

19 "What's the Difference Between a Mentor and a Sponsor?," *Harvard Business Review*, October 21, 2021, https://hbr.

org/2021/10/whats-the-difference-between-a-mentor-and-a-sponsor.

20 Kathy Gurchiek, "Survey: Respect at Work Boosts Job Satisfaction," SHRM, August 16, 2019, https://www.shrm.org/resourcesandtools/hr-topics/employee-relations/pages/2016-job-satisfaction-and-engagement-survey.aspx.

21 "Why Inclusive Leaders Are Good for Organizations, and How to Become One," *Harvard Business Review*, November 30, 2021, https://hbr.org/2019/03/why-inclusive-leaders-are-good-for-organizations-and-how-to-become-one.

22 "How to Make Diversity and Inclusion Real," *Harvard Business Review*, August 27, 2021, https://hbr.org/2011/07/how-to-make-diversity-and-incl.

23 Mellody Hobson, "Color Blind or Color Brave?," TED Talks, May 5, 2014, https://www.ted.com/talks/mellody_hobson_color_blind_or_color_brave?language=en.

24 "Building Economic Opportunity for Black Communities," About Netflix, n.d., https://about.netflix.com/en/news/building-economic-opportunity-for-black-communities.

25 Becca Carnahan, "6 Best Practices to Creating Inclusive and Equitable Interview Processes," *Harvard Business School*, August 16, 2021, https://www.hbs.edu/recruiting/insights-and-advice/blog/post/6-best-practices-to-creating-inclusive-and-equitable-interview-processes.

26 DiversityInc Staff, "PwC's Tim Ryan: Getting Real About Blind Spots," DiversityInc Best Practices, August 14, 2017, https://www.diversityincbestpractices.com/pwcs-tim-ryan-getting-real-blind-spots/.

27 Ellen McGirt, "PwC's Quiet Revolutionary," *Fortune*, June 7, 2021, https://fortune.com/longform/pwc-diversity-tim-ryan/.

28 David Gelles, "'There Is a Bigger Role': A C.E.O. Pushes Diversity," *New York Times*, March 7, 2021, https://www.nytimes.com/2021/03/05/business/tim-ryan-pwc-corner-office.html.

29 "Yahoo Is Part of the Yahoo Family of Brands," n.d., https://www.yahoo.com/video/pete-carroll-seahawks-white-people-real-history-racism-speech-nfl-032543213.html.

30 Denver Nicks, "How Richard Nixon Predicted the Canadian Election," *Time*, October 20, 2015, https://time.com/4079918/justin-trudeau-richard-nixon/.

31 Ben Skipper, "Canada's Feminist Prime Minister Justin Trudeau Targets GamerGate in Anti-Misogyny Call to Action," *International Business Times UK*, October 23, 2015, https://www.ibtimes.co.uk/canadas-feminist-prime-minister-justin-trudeau-targets-gamergate-anti-misogyny-call-action-1525176.

32 Prachi Gupta, "Canada's New Prime Minister Is a Feminist," *Cosmopolitan*, October 20, 2015, https://www.cosmopolitan.com/politics/news/a47964/canadas-prime-minister-feminist/.

33 Anna Purna Kambhampaty, Madeleine Carlisle, and Melissa Chan, "Justin Trudeau Wore Brownface at 2001 'Arabian Nights' Party While He Taught at a Private School," *Time*, September 19, 2019, https://time.com/5680759/justin-trudeau-brownface-photo/.

34 "Statement by the Prime Minister on the National Day for Truth and Reconciliation," Prime Minister of Canada, September 30, 2022, https://pm.gc.ca/en/news/statements/2022/09/30/statement-prime-minister-national-day-truth-and-reconciliation.

35 Katie Reilly, "'Fight Our Tribal Mindset.' Read Justin Trudeau's Commencement Address to NYU Graduates," *Time*, May 17, 2018, https://time.com/5280153/justin-trudeau-nyu-commencement-2018-transcript/.

36 Matt Perez, "Justin Trudeau: 'We All Watch in Horror and Consternation What's Going On in the United States,'" *Forbes*, June 2, 2020, https://www.forbes.com/sites/mattperez/2020/06/02/justin-trudeau-we-all-watch-in-horror-and-consternation-whats-going-on-in-the-united-states/?sh=69ec309a7baf.

37 Richard Branson, "Richard Branson | Foster Diversity, Not Division | Mint," Mint, March 3, 2014, https://www.livemint.com/Opinion/HIVNbMGl3oJuyVh174F1FI/Richard-Branson--Foster-diversity-not-division.html.

38   "Embracing Neurodiversity in Business | Virgin," Virgin.com, September 2, 2021, https://www.virgin.com/branson-family/richard-branson-blog/embracing-neurodiversity-in-business.

39   "Phi Beta Kappa | Voices and Ideas," n.d., https://pbk.olemiss.edu/voices-and-ideas/.

40   Jacqueline Knirnschild, "Former Mississippi Governor Ray Mabus on Education, Racism, and Change," *The Key Reporter*, June 22, 2020, https://pbk.olemiss.edu/voices-and-ideas.

41   "Former Mississippi Governor Ray Mabus Says 'It's Never Too Late,'" *BBC News*, June 11, 2020, https://www.bbc.com/news/av/uk-53015499.

42   "The Secretary of the Navy Is Under Fire for Politicizing Ship Names," *Business Insider*, September 15, 2016, https://www.businessinsider.com/navy-secretary-under-fire-politicizing-ship-names-2016-9?international=true&r=US&IR=T.

43   U.S. Department of Defense, "Navy Secretary, DoD Celebrate Diversity During LGBT Event," n.d., https://www.defense.gov/News/News-Stories/Article/Article/794765/navy-secretary-dod-celebrate-diversity-during-lgbt-event/.

44   "50 Highest Rated CEOs 2013 | Glassdoor," n.d., https://www.glassdoor.com/Award/50-Highest-Rated-CEOs-2013-LST_KQ0,26.htm.

45   "Yahoo Is Part of the Yahoo Family of Brands," n.d., https://www.yahoo.com/news/former-mississippi-gov-every-single-223314136.html.

46   Ibid.

47   *USA Today* Sports, "Roger Goodell on Colin Kaepernick: 'We Believe Very Strongly in Patriotism in the NFL,'" *USA Today*, September 8, 2016, https://eu.usatoday.com/story/sports/nfl/2016/09/07/goodell-doesnt-agree-with-kaepernicks-actions/89958636/.

48   Chuck Schilken, "Seahawks' Michael Bennett on National Anthem Protests: 'You Need a White Guy to Join the Fight,'" *Los Angeles Times*, September 23, 2016, https://www.latimes.com/sports/sportsnow/la-sp-michael-bennett-colin-kaepernick-anthem-20160923-snap-story.html.

49   Nina Mandell et al., "Read Seth DeValve's Powerful Reasons for Kneeling during the National Anthem," For the Win, *USA*

Today, August 22, 2017, https://ftw.usatoday.com/2017/08/seth-devalve-national-anthem-browns.

50 Pat McManamon, "What Cleveland Browns Players Said About National Anthem Kneeling—NFL Nation—ESPN," ESPN.com, August 22, 2017, https://www.espn.com/blog/nflnation/post/_/id/245393/what-browns-players-said-about-kneeling-praying-during-national-anthem.

51 Erica Harris DeValve, "I'm Proud of My Husband for Kneeling During the Anthem, but Don't Make Him a White Savior," *The Root*, August 24, 2017, https://www.theroot.com/i-m-proud-of-my-husband-for-kneeling-during-the-anthem-1798374605.

52 Annie Linskey, Chelsea Janes, and Amy Wang, "Biden Denounces Racial Inequities in Blasting Capitol Riot," *Washington Post*, January 8, 2021, https://www.washingtonpost.com/politics/biden-racial-inequity-capitol-mob/2021/01/07/07d5961e-5112-11eb-b96e-0e54447b23a1_story.html.

Index

About the Author

Colette A. M. Phillips is an iconic cultural change catalyst, DE&I pioneer, thought leader, innovator, practical visionary, influencer, PR and marketing maven, social commentator, philanthropist, serial entrepreneur, and über-connector. She is the President and CEO of Colette Phillips Communications, Inc., and founder of **Get Konnected!** In the midst of the pandemic and America's racial reckoning, she created a **Get Konnected!** business ecosystem to support BIPOC businesses and professionals of color; these initiatives included the groundbreaking **GK! Market** and the **GK Fund**, which were focused on giving exposure, capital, and opportunities for small businesses to grow during the pandemic, and **GK! Execu-Search**, whose competitive advantage is that it is exclusively focused on helping companies diversify both their C-suites and corporate board rooms. In the fall of 2020, her agency was awarded what was at the time the single largest non-construction contract by the City of Boston as the lead agency for the groundbreaking All Inclusive Boston campaign in partnership with Proverb Agency and the Greater Boston Convention & Visitors Bureau. She is a values-based leader and trusted advisor who uses her influence and communications expertise to engage, enlighten, empower, and educate multiple stakeholders on a variety of issues. She has extensive experience advising C-level executives, public figures, world leaders, entrepreneurs, and leadership teams across multiple industries including academia, arts and entertainment, energy, health care, financial services, nonprofit, retail, real estate, sports, technology, and transportation. She is a widely recognized expert in strategy and transformation who is frequently consulted by corporations and nonprofit institutions on how to establish healthy, inclusive working environments for their employees and how to engage and serve culturally diverse consumers and other stakeholders.

A savvy and enterprising risk-taker, she pioneered inclusion and multicultural marketing in New England. She is highly respected for her expertise and ability to create cross-cultural business and social relationships and networks. Boston's Mayor **Michelle Wu** and former Mayors **Kim Janey** and **Marty Walsh** (former Secretary of Labor in the Biden Administration and current Executive Director of the National Hockey Players Association) cite her as one of their invaluable trusted advisors and mentors. She and her communications firm provide strategic public relations and tactical support for stakeholder engagement; diversity, equity, and inclusion consulting; brand activation; reputation and crisis management; multicultural marketing; and executive coaching. Her game-changing insights and her ability to help people bridge differences and connect more meaningfully often result in solving challenging problems with positive social impact outcomes.

She is the recipient of numerous awards and accolades for her personal, philanthropic, and professional accomplishments. She is cited on *Boston* magazine's 2023, 2022, 2020, and 2018 lists of the 100 Most Influential Bostonians. The American Jewish Committee (AJC) of New England honored her with its 2018 Co-Existence Award given to leaders who have contributed to a more peaceful, pluralistic, and democratic world by advancing our collective commitment to coexistence. She was one of fifty individuals including the late Dr. Martin Luther King Jr. who were chosen to adorn a community mural called *Game Changers*. In 2022, 2021, 2017, and 2016, the *Boston Business Journal* listed her on its annual **Power 50** list of the most influential businesspeople in Boston, citing her as a "Movement Builder" and "Game-Changer." *Boston* magazine featured her in 2018 in its "Influencer" column with the subtitle "Who needs LinkedIn when you've got Colette Phillips?" *Boston Globe* named her as an "A-Lister," calling her Boston's "social connector," and one of the "must have" people in the room when there are important events. She is author of *21 Steps for Women to Win*, a compact, inspirational guide for women entrepreneurs and professional women, and is the creator and publisher of *Kaleidoscope*, Boston's first and only multicultural resource directory. She holds a BS and MS from Emerson College and an Honorary Doctor of Law from Mount Ida College.

Colette currently serves on the advisory board of Eastern Bank and the Madison Park Technical Vocational High School; is an honorary trustee for Massachusetts General Hospital; is on the Board of Directors for the Greater Boston Chamber of Commerce, the American Jewish Committee, the Alliance for Business Leadership, and the Commonwealth Institute; is a mentor/advisor for Conexion, a mentoring organization for mid-level Latino professionals; and is a mentor for entrepreneurs who are the grantees of her GK Fund.